ABBA
THE BOOK

ABBA
THE BOOK

JEAN-MARIE POTIEZ

angus

For Stig Anderson – in tribute to his work with ABBA

A QUANTUM BOOK

Published by Angus Books Ltd
Swift Distribution
Units 1 – 6 Kingsnorth Industrial Estate
Hoo, Nr. Rochester
Kent ME3 9ND

This updated edition printed 2007

First published by Aurum Press Ltd, 2000 & 2003

There is a website for ABBA: The Book at: http://abbathebook.online.fr

ISBN 978-1-84573-306-3

QUMA229

This book is produced by
Quantum Publishing Ltd.
6 Blundell Street
London N7 9BH

Design by TWO:design London
Additional illustration by Paul Wright
Printed in Singapore by
Star Standard Industries (Pte) Ltd

contents

Introduction 7

Agnetha 8
Björn 14
Benny 20
Anni-Frid 26
Stig 32
1969 38
1970 44
1971 52
1972 60
1973 72
1974 86
Brighton Fever 96
1974–75 Tour 104
1975 110
1976 124
1977 140
1977 Tour 154
Abba–The Movie 164
1978 170
1979 184
1979 Tour 200
1980 212
1981 224
1982 236
Where Are They Now? 252

Discography 258
Acknowledgements 262
Sources 262
Picture Credits 263

'THE INTERESTING ASPECT OF THE ABBA SOUND WAS CREATED BY OUR DIFFERENCES.'   AGNETHA

'I THINK ALL THE DREAMS I COULD POSSIBLY HAVE WITHIN A POP GROUP HAVE BEEN REALIZED WITH ABBA. NOW I CAN'T THINK OF ANYTHING ELSE!'   BJÖRN

'I WOULD STILL LIKE TO KNOW WHY WE HAD THE SUCCESS WE DID WITH ABBA. BUT I HAVE NO IDEA. I MEAN, WE WROTE GOOD SONGS, WE MADE GOOD RECORDINGS, THE GIRLS ARE GREAT SINGERS ... THAT'S NOT THE REASON FOR IT. THERE IS SOMETHING ELSE WHICH CAN'T BE DEFINED WHICH HAS NOTHING TO DO WITH US IN A WAY.'   BENNY

'THE ABBA YEARS GAVE ME SO MUCH. I'M GLAD AND PROUD OF WHAT WE DID. IT'S NOT A CHAPTER I WANT TO FORGET.' ANNI-FRID

introduction

Abba: The Book could have started with the words 'Once upon a time', as the ABBA story has an almost fairy-tale quality about it. Even if the gods did smile upon Agnetha, Björn, Benny and Anni-Frid at birth, one must not underestimate how hard they worked, nor overlook the fact that their success was due in large part to the alchemy of talent, hard work, charisma, and that indefinable something extra that all great stars possess. And behind ABBA there was Stig Anderson, the man who made it all possible. Without him, the group would certainly not have existed.

When I prepared my documentary Thank You Abba, I met and interviewed Stig at his home in Stockholm. Contrary to what I had been told about him, I found him charming, passionate and generous. He became very emotional as he recalled the career of ABBA and talked of all the things he could have done had the group not broken up. Stig loved France and understood my passion for ABBA. His help, both with the documentary and the preparation of this book, was invaluable. He opened his personal photographic archive to me and recounted at great length the rise of ABBA to international stardom.

This book takes a new approach to the ABBA story. For the first time, the career of each member of the group prior to the formation of ABBA is pieced together. Access to numerous archives has enabled me to retrace their steps, detailing all their activities and tours before and after they came together as ABBA the group, and following the success of ABBA in Scandinavia, the UK and the rest of Europe, Australia and the United States. As a result of exhaustive research, Abba: The Book is the most complete and factually accurate history of ABBA to date. The book is illustrated with many rare and previously unpublished photographs, as well as a number of interesting documents such as record sleeves, advertisements, tickets, newspaper cuttings and magazine covers.

I want this book to be a gift for all the loyal ABBA fans and for all those who want to know more about the musical and personal development of these four extraordinary Swedes. The original fans will be able to explore the complete history of their favourite group in detail, including much previously unpublished information. Others can follow ABBA's fabulous success story day by day, putting in context the numerous dramatic events of their career.

What gives me most pleasure is that each of you, on reading this book, is going to discover – or rediscover – the story and the magic of ABBA.

Happy reading!

Jean-Marie Potiez
Paris, 2000

Agnetha

Agnetha Åse Fältskog, known as Anna in some countries, was born in Jönköping, a town on the shores of Lake Vättern in the south of Sweden, on 5 April 1950. The young girl grew up in a very musical and artistic environment. Her father, Ingvar, had a passion for shows, and regularly put on amateur reviews, sometimes even performing his own sketches on stage. Her mother, Birgit, would often sing at home, but always refused to display her talents in public.

Agnetha was just five years old when she discovered a piano belonging to a neighbour, who was a musician with the town's brass band. The black and white notes fascinated her and the sounds she could make with them captured her imagination. Every day, the little girl would tap away on the keyboard. She dreamed of having a piano of her very own. Two years later, her parents gave her the instrument she so desperately wanted. At the same time, Agnetha made her début on stage. Her father asked her to sing at a Christmas party, and in front of an audience consisting mainly of elderly people, she sang 'Billy Boy'. Her trousers fell down in the middle of the song, causing a great deal of hilarity, but this didn't diminish her passion for the stage.

The family grew: Mrs Fältskog gave birth to a girl, who was named Mona. During her spare time, Agnetha looked after her sister and took piano lessons, supported by her father, who was very proud of his talented daughter. Despite having some difficulties co-ordinating both hands on the keyboard, Agnetha very soon developed a particular gift for composition. She gave her first little song the title 'Två Små Troll' (Two Little Trolls).

As time passed, Agnetha filled numerous exercise books with her own lyrics and melodies. In the classroom, she had no interest at all in mathematics, physics or chemistry. On the other hand, she was very gifted where languages and music were concerned. With her two best friends, Elisabeth and Lena, she formed a vocal trio called the Cambers. The encouragement given to the group at local shows prompted them to send a cassette to Swedish Radio. They received a brutal response: 'No thank you!' Agnetha abandoned the Cambers and continued her stage apprenticeship in her father's shows. Alone in her room, she spent hours listening to and studying the songs of her idol, Connie Francis.

'CONNIE FRANCIS WAS MY GREAT IDOL. SHE WAS EASY TO IMITATE, IN SONGS SUCH AS "WHO'S SORRY NOW?" AND "MY HAPPINESS", IN FRONT OF THE LITTLE MIRROR IN MY ROOM. I'D LISTEN FOR HOURS ON END, ETCHING THE WORDS, MUSIC AND TIMBRE INTO MY MIND. I TAUGHT MYSELF THE PHRASING, AND TO BREATHE IN EXACTLY THE SAME MANNER AS CONNIE.'
AGNETHA

However, despite having an angelic face and a romantic image, the young singer became the object of some serious attacks in the press. Her new single 'Zigenarvän' (Gypsy Friend) caused a scandal. The song, recalling the legend of the gypsies, found itself at the centre of a controversy which was dividing Sweden at the time. The Swedish government was debating the problems of integrating gypsies, and Agnetha became the target of racist remarks, to which she replied: 'I'm sorry that people think like that. I wrote the music to go with Bengt Haslum's lyrics. It's just the story of a young girl who falls in love with a gypsy!'

The following year, Danish musician Per Hviid accused the singer of having plagiarized one of his melodies in the song 'Om Tårar Vore Guld' (If Tears Were Made of Gold). The composer claimed that Agnetha would have heard his song when he was touring Sweden. He lost all credibility when it was discovered that the tour took place in 1950, the year of the singer's birth.

These attacks, commercial failure in Germany, and the break-up with her fiancé all began to take their toll on Agnetha, and she started to doubt herself. However, clearly her guardian angel was at hand, for at the beginning of May, a chance meeting was to completely transform her life and career.

' "JAG VAR SÅ KÄR" (I WAS SO IN LOVE) WAS MY FIRST SINGLE... I REMEMBER THAT IT BECAME No.3 IN THE SVENSKTOPPEN AND No.1 IN THE KVÄLLSTOPPEN IN 1968, JUST BEFORE THE BEATLES.'
AGNETHA

Agnetha Fältskog

Agnetha FÄLTSKOG

ALLTING HAR FÖRÄNDRAT SEJ
DEN JAG VÄNTAT PÅ

FÖLJ MED MIG · JAG VAR SÅ KÄR

Cupol

agnetha fältskog
och jörgen edman

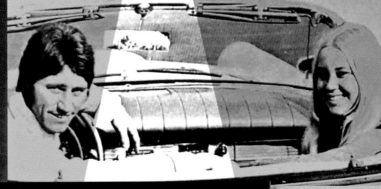

CS 233

AGNETHA
FÄLTSKOG

Marcus Österdahls orkester

EN
SOMMAR
MED DIG

FÖRSONADE

Cupol   STEREO
         även spelbar i
         MONO

AGNETHA
FÄLTSKOG

Snövit
och de 7 dwärgarna

agnetha
fältsko

SLUTET GOTT,
ALLTING GOTT

UTAN DEJ

Cupol

Björn

Björn Christian Ulvaeus was born on 25 April 1945 in Gothenburg, Sweden's second city, on the country's west coast. In 1951, the family moved to the small town of Västervik, on the east coast. His mother, Aina, and father, Gunnar, both loved music, and they gave Björn his first guitar on his eleventh birthday. He quickly got used to the instrument, learning some chords with his cousin, Jon Ulfsäter, and was soon beginning to try his hand at jazz and folk. Even though he was showing a great talent for music, the teenager continued his studies in law, following the advice of his parents.

At university, Björn and his friend Tony Rooth met two other musicians, Hansi Schwarz and Johan Karlberg, and soon the West Bay Singers were born. Encouraged by their music teacher, Lars Frosterud, the group put together a repertoire mainly inspired by the idols of the time – the Kingston Trio and the Brothers Four. The four students shared a passion for folk music and Dixieland jazz. The West Bay Singers became popular in the Västervik area, and after taking part in an amateur competition held in the neighbouring town of Gamleby, they decided to set off to conquer Europe.

In 1963, they borrowed an old Volvo, packed their instruments and left to launch an attack on the neighbouring countries. Even if their performances didn't leave much of a mark in the annals of rock history, the experience taught them a lot and the four boys managed to earn enough to pay for their food and lodging without any difficulty. The trip ended in Spain.

On their return to Sweden, a surprise awaited them. The West Bay Singers' number-one fan, Björn's mother, had entered her young protégés for a national talent show, *Plats På Scen* (Place On the Stage), organized by Swedish Radio during the autumn. 'I was stunned when my mother told me the news,' Björn recalls. 'I wanted to cancel our appearance straight away, because I thought that we weren't ready. And then finally, after some thought, I told myself that maybe we had a chance. Our name sounded good and fitted our repertoire perfectly.' The group were successful in the quarter- and semi-finals and then travelled to Norrköping for the final of the competition. There were seven finalists, and despite a good performance, the West Bay Singers were not among the prizewinners. (Interestingly, Anni-Frid Lyngstad also took part in the competition.)

Defeat was difficult to accept. However, fate intervened: Bengt Bernhag, a talent scout who had recently teamed up with publisher-composer-producer Stig Anderson, read an article about the competition and was instantly attracted by the name 'West Bay Singers'. Bengt and Stig were at that time looking for a group who would be able to sing folk music in Swedish. Discreet, polite and intuitive, Bengt had always had a flair for discovering new talent; he had successfully produced records for an ageing trumpet player who had lost his popularity, and had managed to push two female singers whom

'LENNON AND McCARTNEY WERE THE REASON WHY BENNY AND I STARTED WRITING. BEFORE THE BEATLES, NEITHER OF US HAD WRITTEN ANYTHING.' **BJÖRN**

'I LIKED BENNY INSTANTLY.
HE WAS OBVIOUSLY TALENTED
AND I FOUND HIM EASY TO
TALK TO. WE BOTH HAD THIS
LOVE OF MUSIC AND HAD
MUCH THE SAME TASTES.'
BJÖRN

everyone had described as 'untalented' up to the No. 1 spot in the charts. He had such good judgement that once he had mentioned the West Bay Singers to Stig, the latter didn't take much persuading. Bengt asked the group to send in a demo tape. 'We were certainly convincing,' Björn believes. 'Technically, the songs were perfect, since we'd recorded in a radio studio in Västervik. One of the songs was called "Ave Maria, No Morro". Bengt and Stig invited us for an audition in Stockholm. We were very excited to have the opportunity to sing in front of them. They immediately put us at ease. I think our performance was satisfactory.' Stig added: 'Bengt and myself sat down. What we heard was fantastic. The four of them made up a homogeneous group and their voices blended perfectly. I must confess that when I saw Björn singing and playing, I had a feeling that he had enormous potential. They were a good group, of course, but Björn stood out from the others. They were the first artists to be signed to our new Polar label. I set them two conditions: I wanted them to begin their career by singing in Swedish, and they had to change their name. "West Bay Singers" was old-fashioned. With a name like that I couldn't see them reaching No. 1 in the charts, even if [the name] was the English translation of their home town, Västervik.'

Stig thought it would be original to call the group 'The Hootenanny Singers', which loosely translated means 'meeting of folk singers'. With their name, their appearance and their repertoire, they seemed quite exotic in the Swedish Top 20. It was still rare for Swedish artists to sing in their mother tongue. Visually, they were also different from other groups: they had impeccable haircuts and always wore three-piece suits, both when they appeared on stage and on television. Although it ran contrary to fashion at that time, Stig and Bengt were right: the Hootenanny Singers' first single, 'Jag Väntar Vid Min Mila' (I'm Waiting By My Pile of Coal), beat other young talents to win a TV contest and went on to crush any competition in the Swedish charts. The song was a cover version of a very old Swedish ballad.

On 27 February 1964, the Hootenanny Singers gave their first concert at the Bromma high school, near Stockholm. The event was recorded by Swedish Radio. After releasing their first single, the group recorded an album of six songs in Swedish and six in English. They would always maintain this combination of songs in both languages, alternating cover versions and original compositions. Also, singing in English allowed them to attract a younger audience. Björn, influenced by the 'Liverpool Four', sometimes proposed songs in the style of the Beatles, but his three fellow band members always preferred a more traditional repertoire.

Björn, Tony, Johan and Hansi were not carried away by their new career; they continued with their studies and passed their exams in the spring of 1964.

The day after the exams, they were on the road. Their first summer tour started in Timmernabben park, near Oskarshamn. 'I haven't got good memories of those first concerts,' says Björn. 'The sound wasn't that good. We had brought our own instruments and we only had a small amplifier. To transport the equipment, one of us had borrowed a Volvo. The travelling was very tiring because we spent a lot of time on the road. All the weeks on tour taught us what to avoid for future shows.'

Between 1964 and 1966, the Hootenanny Singers went from strength to strength in Sweden. The summer months were dedicated to touring, while they spent the winter months in the recording studio or making television appearances. The group performed in Scandinavia and in Germany, and attempted a breakthrough in countries like England and the United States, using the name 'The Northern Lights'. In 1965, the single 'No Time' appeared in the South African charts. Even if their fame didn't reach beyond the borders of Scandinavia, the Hootenanny Singers were certainly a valuable commodity in Sweden. With their album *Evert Taube På Vårt Sätt* (Evert Taube – Our Way), dedicated to the Swedish poet Evert Taube, they really hit the big time.

The Hootenanny Singers seemed quite exotic in the Swedish Top 20

'THE FIRST YEARS IN THE PARKS WERE USEFUL IN THEIR WAY. I KNOW TODAY EXACTLY THE CONDITIONS IN WHICH ONE SHOULD NOT WORK. EVERYTHING WAS WRONG. THERE WAS NO POSSIBILITY OF GIVING THE AUDIENCE THE KIND OF SOUND THEY HAVE A RIGHT TO EXPECT.' BJÖRN

In 1966, the singles 'Björkens Visa' (Song of the Birch Tree), 'Baby Those Are the Rules' and the album *Många Ansikten* (Many Faces) also sold well. However, pessimists predicted the end of the group when, after managing to postpone it for several years, Björn, Johan and Tony announced that they would be doing their national service. However, the Hootenanny Singers were able to continue with their career during their military service, often appearing on stage and recording new songs.

On 5 June 1966, a fortunate coincidence occurred: the bus carrying Benny's group, the Hep Stars, and the one belonging to the Hootenanny Singers met at a crossroads in the countryside. The Hootenanny Singers were going to Linköping to appear at a party. Björn invited the Hep Stars to join them after the concert, and late that night, the two groups met up. Björn and Benny got on instantly, and it wasn't long before they started strumming their guitars, playing Beatles songs together.

Several weeks later, another meeting would seal their friendship: the paths of the two groups crossed again at a concert in Västervik, Björn's home town. At the end of their performances, Benny and Björn met up in the motel bar. Over a few beers, they joked, exchanged stories and industry gossip and finally fell into a serious discussion about their real passion: music. 'We had the same musical tastes,' says Björn. 'When Benny started speaking, our ideas were so similar that it was like I was listening to myself. We both thought that from now on it would be good to write all the material for our respective groups. Playing other people's material wasn't enough for us. We even started to write a song that very night!' Björn took Benny home to work in the basement of his parents' house, but their collaboration was soon interrupted by Björn's father. Woken by the noise, he came down to suggest they continue playing their music at his paper mill!

By daybreak, 'Isn't It Easy To Say', the first Ulvaeus/Andersson song had been written, and a new songwriting team was born. The song was recorded during the autumn of 1966 by the Hep Stars (with Björn on guitar) and included on the album *Hep Stars*.

At the same time, the Hootenanny Singers hired Benny for sessions on the song 'Blomman' (The Flower), featured on the *Många Ansikten* (Many Faces) album. Björn even joined the Hep Stars on stage on 26 December at the Härnösand's *folkets park*, standing in at the last minute for guitarist Janne Frisck, who was held up in Spain.

The following year, the Hootenanny Singers had one of their biggest hits with a song called 'En Sång, En Gång För Längesen' (A Song, Once Upon a Time, a Long Time Ago), the Swedish version of Tom Jones's hit 'Green Green Grass of Home'.

During the autumn of 1967, Björn went through a period of uncertainty about his future, and he returned to his studies in law and economics at the University of Stockholm. Hansi prepared a thesis at the University of Lund, Johan worked in Vimmerby, his birthplace, and Tony, who had just married, studied psychology at Lund.

Fortunately, this period of hesitation was short-lived. Björn had always had a flair for studying, but this time he found he had lost his passion for his college course. Lately, he had been working with Stig and Bengt in their music-publishing company. This side of the business really interested him more than anything else, and he made his mind up to learn the trade. However, he hadn't realized how determined Bengt and Stig could be. Both of them knew from the start that Björn's future lay on stage, not behind a desk; Stig was certain that one day Björn would have an international music career. After long discussions, the two men managed to convince him to carry on with composing and recording. He eventually left university when Benny phoned to ask if he could again stand in for guitarist Janne Frisck.

In February 1968, the Hootenanny Singers were in Saalbach, Austria, where they put the finishing touches to the songs for the new album, *Bellman På Vårt Sätt* (Bellman – Our Way). During breaks, the members of the group were able to go skiing. While waiting in the queue for the ski-lift, Björn exchanged glances with Marianne Åkerman, a pretty young Swede on holiday. The attraction was mutual, and Björn said later to the magazine *Bild Journalen*: 'Don't write that we are engaged. For the moment, we are very happy together. We go to restaurants and to the cinema, but there is nothing more between us.'

In April 1968, Björn recorded his first solo single called 'Raring' (Darling). The song was the Swedish version of the American hit 'Honey', by Bobby Goldsboro. The lyrics were written by Stig Anderson. Three other singles sung by Björn were to follow: 'Fröken Fredriksson' (Miss Fredriksson) in the same year and, in 1969, 'Saknar Du Något Min Kära?' (Do You Regret Anything My Dear?) and 'Partaj-Aj-Aj'.

On 21 December, the Hootenanny Singers left Gothenburg for the Caribbean; they had been invited to perform during a month-long cruise. The musicians were accompanied by their wives; in Björn's case, by his sister.

Between 1966 and 1968, Björn and Benny were completely involved with touring and recording with their respective groups and had little time to write anything together, apart from a second song at the end of October 1968, 'A Flower In My Garden', produced by Bengt Palmers. Björn played guitar on this song, which featured as the B-side of the Hep Stars' 'Holiday For Clowns' single.

Björn met Marianne in Saalbach, Austria

Björn with his parents Gunnar & Aina

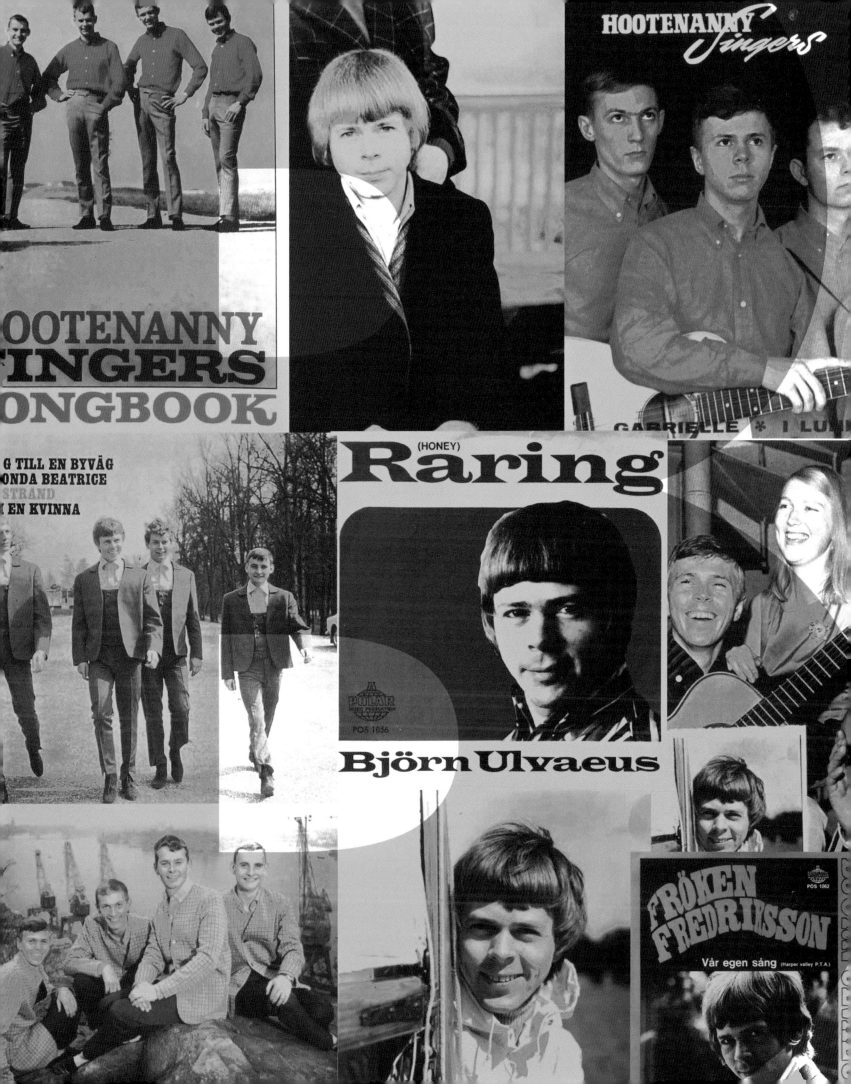

'I GREW UP ON ACCORDION MUSIC FROM THE AGE OF SIX AND THEN CAME ELVIS PRESLEY AND CATERINA VALENTE, THEN THERE WAS A LITTLE BIT OF MANTOVANI AND EDVARD GRIEG.' **BENNY**

Benny

Göran Bror Benny Andersson was born on 16 December 1946 in the Vasastaden district of Stockholm. The Andersson family moved to Vällingby, a town to the west of the Swedish capital, two years after his birth. It could be said that this child was born into music, as the Anderssons would often get together to sing and play.

Encouraged by his father, Gösta, and his grandfather, Efraim, young Benny advanced quickly. He was already playing the accordion at the age of six. The two men taught him not only musical technique, but also ancient Swedish folk songs. The first piece of music that the child learned to play by heart was called 'Där Näckrosen Blommar' (Where the Water Lilies Bloom). During the summer months, Benny would accompany his elders on the accordion at family celebrations. He was very talented and had soon completely mastered the instrument.

At the age of ten, Benny was given a piano. It was a revelation: 'Despite the fact that the first piano lessons I had at school were off-putting, I immediately felt that it was my instrument. Step by step, I developed my own way of playing. I never wanted to learn musical theory. As far as I'm concerned, the whole point of music is for it to be something you enjoy and not something you're forced to do. This passion has always been with me. Even today, whenever I see a piano, I can't help playing it!'

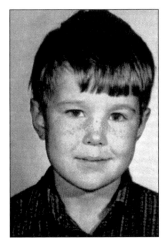

At fifteen, Benny left school. He wasn't really keen on studying, much preferring to listen to beautiful melodies and pop music. After having tried his hand at selling washing machines door to door for three weeks, he landed a job as a caretaker. In the evenings, he played in a club near where he lived, sometimes accompanied by a young singer called Christina Grönvall. The two teenagers became inseparable and fell in love. On 20 August 1963, Christina gave birth to a son, Peter.

At this time, Benny became the keyboard player with a local group, the Elverkets Spelmanslag, who regularly performed in the Vällingby area. It was here that things started to develop. The group got a contract to perform a long way from Stockholm and were forced to borrow a van from Svenne Hedlund, the singer with another local group, the Hep Stars. Svenne offered to take them to the venue at the *folkets park* in Virserum. He was present at the performance and noticed Benny's dexterity on the keyboards. Some months later, in October 1964, Hans Östlund, the Hep Stars' keyboard player, left the group, and Svenne offered the job to Benny, who accepted without hesitation. Svenne remembers: 'The funniest thing was that Benny stood out from the start. He had a perfect crew cut and wore a tie, while the

'I SOON REALIZED THAT THE PIANO WAS GOING TO BE MY INSTRUMENT. FATHER AND GRANDFATHER TAUGHT ME EVERYTHING. I HAVE VIRTUALLY NEVER TAKEN MUSIC LESSONS. I HAD TWO OR THREE PIANO LESSONS AT SCHOOL, BUT I THOUGHT THEY WERE DULL.' **BENNY**

In 1969, one of their compositions, 'Hej Clown' (Hello Clown), was performed by Jan Malmsjö in the Melodifestivalen (the selection of the song to represent Sweden at the Eurovision Song Contest), but it was not chosen to go forward to the final.

The incredible career of the Hep Stars continued. They became national idols. However, even if every record sold more than 100,000 copies (an enormous figure for a small country like Sweden), they still lacked a proper manager. In a joint decision, they decided to create their own publishing and production company, called Hep House, but musicians do not necessarily make good businessmen. Nothing was managed properly, and money was going out faster than it was coming in.

The Hep Stars launched headlong into filming a musical entitled *Habari-Safari*. The group went off to Africa for two weeks with a film crew. The director, Åke Borglund, and the manager of Hep House made the most of the trip and gave themselves an extra week's holiday at the expense of the group. Added to the already large bill were ten days of filming in Denmark, as well as the cost of hiring a private plane to take the group to London to record in a Soho studio.

On their return, it became clear that what had been shot was unuseable. They had neither a story nor a main theme. It was then that things suddenly began to fall apart. It emerged that nobody had ever declared any income to the taxman, and the amount outstanding was more than a million Swedish crowns. In December 1967, the newspapers exposed the 'Hep Stars scandal'. Faced with these debts, the musicians became disillusioned. In July 1968, Hep House Productions was declared bankrupt, and each member of the group had to pay back their share.

For Benny, this was a bitter pill; from now on he would have to work without ever seeing a penny of his earnings. In two years, his income dropped from 174,000 to 8,000 kronor. However, he managed to repay his debts fairly quickly. But the Hep Stars' troubles were by no means over: a further demand for 83,000 kronor arrived, relating to earnings for 1968. Things were no longer going well within the group. The creative atmosphere and the motivation had gone. Guitarist Janne Frisck left at the end of February 1969. He was temporarily replaced for the duration of a tour by Björn Ulvaeus.

' I DON'T HAVE A BROTHER BUT BJÖRN IS MY BROTHER. NOTHING WILL ALTER THE FACT THAT WE ARE TRUE FRIENDS. AS WITH A BROTHER, ANYTHING COULD HAPPEN AND HE WOULD STILL BE TO ME WHAT HE HAS ALWAYS BEEN.' **BENNY**

Anni-Frid

Ballangen is a small Norwegian village situated about 35 kilometres to the west of Narvik. In 1945, the country was still occupied by German troops, whose brutal methods aroused both fear and hatred among the Norwegians. However, nineteen-year-old Synni Lyngstad had befriended a non-commissioned officer, Alfred Haase, six years her senior. Gradually, the bond between them grew deeper and they fell in love. Synni didn't think of him as a uniformed enemy soldier. All she could see was a man far from home, forced to fulfil a duty he detested. Despite warnings from her friends and family, Synni continued to see Alfred in secret. However, their affair soon became common knowledge all over the village and fingers began to point.

Their happiness was short-lived, as the end of the war meant that the troops began to leave the country. Alfred had to return to Germany, but he promised Synni he would come back as soon as he could. The young woman didn't dare to tell him that she was pregnant, and Alfred didn't admit to her that he was married. His wife was waiting for him in Karlsruhe.

Alfred Haase

Synni Lyngstad

When Synni felt her first contractions on 15 November 1945, the midwife was sick and her replacement didn't arrive in time. The young woman, helped by her mother, Agny, and her sister, Olive, gave birth to a little girl, who she named Anni-Frid. The inhabitants of Ballangen gave her the nickname 'German child', and people would spit, shout insults at her or cross the street when they saw the young mother coming. Synni couldn't care less – her child was more important to her than anything else. She still believed that Alfred would return, and even if her letters remained unanswered, she could always live in hope. Her mother, her four sisters and her brother were there to look out for her, so she wasn't alone, but life was difficult for the young mother and her child. Eventually, Synni and her mother decided to leave town.

Synni found work in a hotel in the region of Hardanger, in the south, and left Anni-Frid in the care of her mother. Some time later, Agny and Anni-Frid crossed the Swedish border and stayed temporarily in Härjedalen before settling in Torshälla, a small town 7 kilometres from Eskilstuna. Agny rented a small two-room flat and worked as a dressmaker. When money was short at the end of the month, she would work washing dishes in a café.

Far from her family and daughter, and still with no news from Alfred, Synni could stand it no longer. She left her job and Norway, and rejoined her family in Torshälla where she found a job as a waitress. Sadly, after several months, she became seriously ill. Before she died, she made her mother promise to take care of Anni-Frid. Synni died in hospital in Flen in September 1947. She was just twenty-one years old.

Anni-Frid with her grandmother Agny

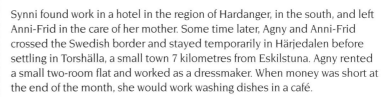

'MY MOTHER WAS ONLY TWENTY-ONE, SHE WAS REALLY PRETTY AND SHE HAD A BEAUTIFUL SINGING VOICE. THAT'S ALL I KNOW. WHEN I WAS YOUNGER, I OFTEN IMAGINED HOW MY PARENTS WERE.' **FRIDA**

600 people. The tour would take them to about forty towns. On stage, they were accompanied by Bengt Hallberg (piano) and his musicians: Rune Gustafsson (guitar), Ronnie Pettersson (bass) and Rune Carlsson (drums). Lars Lönndahl remembers: 'I really enjoyed working with Frida. She was just starting out in the business but was already very professional. She had lots of charisma. She always has had, in fact. She had this natural grace and elegance which wasn't affected. You knew that she was going to be someone. Do you know that at that time she still made her own stage clothes?'

Anni-Frid seems to have enjoyed this first tour: 'Despite long days on the road, I've always enjoyed doing shows. It was hard work but I learned a lot from it. At the time, I was living like those were the best days of my life. It has to be said that Sweden is a beautiful country, especially in the summer. What I missed most of all was my children. I was far away from them and I rarely saw them. Their father was very important during that period. I was lucky to have such an understanding husband. He considered my career to be important and never blamed me for anything.' The tour concluded on 30 June.

Anni-Frid still hadn't had a record in the charts. Was it because her songs were a bit too 'jazzy' and not 'poppy' enough? She was held in high esteem by a lot of people in the music industry, but critics said that she had a limited audience. Yet the young woman was a big hit whenever she appeared on stage and was considered one of the best singers in the country.

It was now 1969, and Frida was spending a lot of time away from her family. Despite missing her children, the young woman decided to move to Bro, north-west of Stockholm, so that she could devote more time to her musical activities. 'I was violently criticized at the time. I was accused of abandoning my family just because I wanted to see my name up in lights. I had considered bringing my children with me to live in Stockholm, but my flat was too tiny and I would have been constantly absent. I really made the right choice. Hans and Lise-Lotte were better off with their father, in our house in Eskilstuna, rather than in my tiny home in the capital. People were very cruel; no one could have imagined how much this decision broke my heart. The worst thing was that when I was on my own at home, I would spend all my time thinking about them. In public, I always tried to hide my pain. My smile concealed a deep sadness.'

Anni-Frid went back to Eskilstuna whenever her timetable permitted. 'It was a real joy to see my children again. On the other hand, Ragnar and myself didn't have anything to say to each other any more. The spark had gone. So, we decided on an amicable divorce. In retrospect, I think we got married when we were too young, without really realizing what life as a couple was all about. The children stayed with him, which was better for everyone.'

Lasse Lönndahl & Anni-Frid on tour, 1968

The Anni-Frid Four was born

Anni-Frid & Agnetha on the Studio 8 TV show

Malmkvist i 'Studio 8'

'En Ledig Dag', Skansen park, 3 September 1967

ANNI-FRID
LYNGSTAD

En ledig dag

Peter, kom tillbaka

XPRESSEN

EMI SVENSKA AB
Box 1289, 171 25 Solna

ANNI-FRID LYNGSTAD

EMI SVENSKA AB
Box 1289, 171 25 Solna

'HE WAS ONE OF THE FIRST MUSIC PUBLISHERS TO DEVELOP WORLDWIDE. HE WAS ALSO KIND-HEARTED – A HUMANIST IN THE FULL SENSE OF THE WORD.' **QUINCY JONES**

Stig

Stig Erik Leopold Anderson was born in the Mariestad maternity hospital on 25 January 1931. His mother, Ester, lived alone in the village of Hova, halfway between Laxå and Mariestad, in the Västergötland region of Sweden. It was difficult being a single mother in those days, and Ester was often the subject of spiteful gossip, but she was a strong woman and wasn't afraid of hard work. She was a hairdresser during the day and made ends meet by taking in people's washing and ironing. Every Friday, she would cycle the 20 kilometres to Finnerödja, where she worked in a sweet shop. 'I used to sit on the basket on the bike,' remembered Stig. 'I was really scared crossing the huge dark forest at night. The reflection from the light used to dart about on the stony road and I used to look up at the sky to make myself feel better. You used to hear terrible stories about the robbers who were around!'

Stig never knew his father. He learned at a very early age that you had to work hard to succeed in life. 'At the age of eleven, I used to get up an hour before my classmates to light the coal stove at our school. I would earn 5 kronor for doing that. Sometimes there was a lot of smoke and I had to clear the air before the other school kids arrived.'

Stig left school when he was thirteen and started work as a delivery boy for Källéns Diversehandel, a grocery store. 'I used to earn 5 kronor a week,' he said. 'It was more of an encouragement than a salary, but it wasn't enough for me.' Stig then got himself a job with the Hova Sports Association in Movallen, where he was responsible for all the equipment. 'I used to wash the players' kits, tidy the changing rooms and paint the lines on the pitch. Every Sunday I would run the sweets and drinks kiosk during the match. Källéns Diversehandel used to give me special prices on what I sold. Sometimes I could earn up to 30 kronor on some matches.'

'STIG IS ONE OF THE BEST PEOPLE I KNOW. ONE HUNDRED PER CENT HONEST. HE IS VERY INTELLIGENT AND ALWAYS KNOWS HOW THINGS SHOULD BE. I GET MAD WHEN THEY TREAT HIM UNFAIRLY ON TV. THEY PAINT HIM THAT WAY JUST BECAUSE THEY WANT HIM THAT WAY.' **FRIDA** IN 1977

'STIG WAS VERY IMPORTANT. HE WAS THE ONE WHO FIRST BELIEVED IN BENNY AND ME AS SONGWRITERS. AT THE BEGINNING OF THE SEVENTIES, HE TOLD US: "ONE DAY, YOU'LL HAVE A WORLDWIDE HIT!" WE WORKED CLOSELY TOGETHER AND HE HAD AN ENORMOUS INFLUENCE.' **BJÖRN**

Stig, Gudrun & their children, Marie & Lars

In 1967, Stig produced the single 'Jag Tror På Sommaren' (I Believe In Summer), sung by Mats Olin, which became the big hit of the summer. At one point, he had six songs in the Svensktoppen Top 10 at the same time. Some said that everything he touched turned to gold. 'Obviously I worked hard,' says Stig. 'During the day, I took care of the day-to-day business in the office, and during the evening, I wrote lyrics to my songs. At night, I kept in contact with my foreign correspondents. That's how I worked, without a secretary, for eight years.'

The secretary who would help Stig and Gudrun with administration was Görel Johnsen. She began working for Sweden Music on 8 September 1969. Görel came from Skultorp, near Skövde, in the west of Sweden, and replied to an advert which read: 'Music-publishing company seeks secretary with a good knowledge of English. Call Gudrun Anderson or Ove Hansson.' The young lady, whose dream was to teach either languages or history, knew nothing about show-business and had never heard of Stig Anderson. Nevertheless, she was given an interview by Gudrun, as Stig was in the United States. 'When I met Gudrun, I immediately felt relaxed,' says Görel. 'She was calm, reassuring, and had a kind look about her. She was used to young people. I was a student and a country girl and Stig would never have given me the job if he had interviewed me!'

'BENNY AND I DIDN'T HAVE MUCH TROUBLE WORKING WITH HIM. BUT THEN, WE SORT OF GREW APART BECAUSE HIS TIME WAS MORE AND MORE OCCUPIED BY BUSINESS.' BJÖRN

Stig bought two small properties, including a ground-floor flat at 18 Jungfrugatan for the new offices of Polar Music/Sweden Music. The company now had seven staff: Stig, Gudrun, Görel, Bengt Bernhag, Ove Hansson, Leif Karlsson and Rolf Lönberg. It was around this time that Björn Ulvaeus and his friend Benny Andersson began writing songs for the other Polar Music artists. Stig recalls the day that Björn introduced him to Benny: 'When the two of them arrived at the office, I really couldn't see what they could have in common because they had such different personalities. Björn tried to convince me to take him on. I said why not, because it wouldn't cost anything to try it out. As soon as I heard the first demos they'd made, I realized that there was a real magic in some parts of their songs. That was only the start, but you could immediately feel that the two of them worked incredibly well together. There was a feeling of ease and lightness in their work.'

With the first musical successes of the Björn Ulvaeus/Benny Andersson partnership, Stig realized he had found a promising team. He said: 'I very quickly made a promise to Björn and Benny that with my help, they would be able to carve out an important place for themselves internationally.' And that is exactly what happened.

Starting from nothing, Stig slowly built up the Polar Music empire through sheer courage, hard work and talent. But if Stig was an emperor, he was far from being a dictator as, apart from a few exceptions, he always made important decisions together with Björn and Benny. Stig also knew how to surround himself with an efficient team. The team that worked around him and ABBA were more like a family unit than employees – even his daughter Marie would later join the team.

To sum up the man and his philosophy of life, here are the four principles he always gave when asked the secret of his success:

- Always work hard

- Give your best

- Don't ever forget anything

- Don't take life too seriously

Björn, Gudrun & Stig

'I'M A GOOD ORGANIZER, I'VE GOT A FEELING FOR MARKETING AND I CAN HEAR IF A SONG IS A GOOD ONE OR A BAD ONE. BUT I ALSO HAVE BUSINESS SENSE.' **STIG**

'MOST OF THE TIME, I DON'T WRITE THE SWEDISH LYRICS MYSELF, BECAUSE I HAVE THE FEELING THAT THEY ARE NOT RIGHT. BUT WHEN I WRITE A SONG, I ALWAYS WRITE ORIGINAL LYRICS IN ENGLISH. THE SWEDISH VERSION IS OFTEN ITS TRANSLATION.' AGNETHA

1969

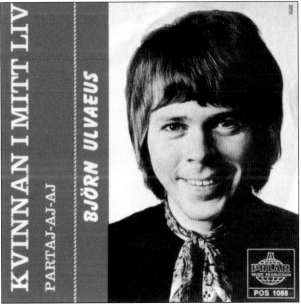

At the beginning of 1969, Johan Karlberg left the Hootenanny Singers to devote all his time to the family firm. Johan said: 'I don't want to be performing on stage at folk parks all my life. I have other ambitions. At the beginning, the popularity was fun. In recent years, it has become a burden!'

This demotivated the group somewhat, and their career seemed to slow down as a result. Björn, for his part, could now get more involved with working with Benny and also concentrate on his solo career. He was single again: his relationship with Marianne Åkerman had just ended.

6 January Agnetha was one of twenty-two artists and groups to perform at the Apollonia in Stockholm before an audience consisting mainly of concert organizers. Agnetha also sponsored a new talent, the young singer Hans Smedberg.

8 January Anni-Frid Lyngstad was on stage at the Valand club in Gothenburg, together with Charlie Norman and his musicians. The Charlie Norman Show played there until the end of the month.

Benny meets Anni-Frid

On 1 February 1969, the Hep Stars began their tour of Sweden's biggest clubs at the Hamburger Börs in Stockholm. At the end of the month, however, guitarist Janne Frisck left the group for good to run a restaurant in Torremolinos. Björn Ulvaeus replaced him for ten days or so. The tour brought them to the Arkaden club in Malmö from 4 to 6 March.

After a concert, Benny went to the Kocksa Krogen bar for a drink and happened to bump into Anni-Frid. The singer was appearing at the Ambassadeur club with Charlie Norman. 'Our meeting wasn't really memorable,' Anni-Frid remembers. 'We talked about our work and about life on the road, but it wasn't a very interesting conversation. We had a drink together and went our separate ways without imagining for a second that we would see each other again a few weeks later.'

Fate would bring them together again on 31 March in Stockholm for the recording of the radio programme Midnight Hour; Anni-Frid and Benny were both members of a jury called Flip Eller Flop. At the end of the programme, Benny asked the singer to join him at a restaurant. 'We found that we had a lot of things in common,' says Anni-Frid. 'Benny was going through a difficult time like myself. That's what brought us together. We talked for hours. We had very different, but complimentary, personalities. He came into my life at the right time, I think, because I was really beginning to doubt everything. I was all alone and depressed in my flat and far away from my children. So much so that I sometimes wondered if my work was really worth all these sacrifices. Benny brought me the comfort that I needed. From that moment on, we were always together.'

1 March Anni-Frid took part in the Melodifestivalen, organized by Swedish Television at the Cirkus in Stockholm. In Sweden, the Melodifestivalen is a real institution and one of the most important television events of the year, watched by more than half the population of Sweden. Pekka Langer presented the ten candidates competing to represent Sweden at the Eurovision Song Contest. Anni-Frid Lyngstad sang 'Härlig Är Vår Jord' (Our World Is Wonderful), wearing a yellow tunic with a black trim.

'THE BEST THING THAT EVER HAPPENED TO ME WAS BENNY, NOT ABBA.' **FRIDA**

Anni-Frid & Benny were officially engaged in August 1969

'WHEN WE STARTED WRITING, I'D SAY BRIAN WILSON WAS MY BIGGEST SOURCE OF INSPIRATION, BECAUSE HE HAS DONE EXACTLY WHAT I THINK WE'RE TRYING TO DO – DOING IT ALL.' BENNY

Lennie Norman & Anni-Frid on stage in *The Charlie Norman Show*

Anni-Frid with Sacha Distel

Her song was well received by the audience. However, the jury chose Tommy Körberg, with his song 'Judy, Min Vän' (Judy, My Friend). Anni-Frid received only 8 points and finished in joint-fourth position with singer Ann-Louise Hanson. Göran Sellgren wrote in the newspaper *Dagens Nyheter*: 'A beautiful young woman with a beautiful song. Anni-Frid's performance was rare in this kind of competition. Her song – a bossa-nova number – was lovely and wasn't at all lacking in personality. Unfortunately, the song isn't memorable, even though the arrangement was very good.' Thanks to 'Härlig Är Vår Jord', Anni-Frid entered the Svensktoppen for the first time on 27 April and reached No. 8.

5 March Swedish singer Brita Borg recorded 'Ljuva Sextital' (Sweet Sixties), one of Björn and Benny's compositions. The lyrics for this song, which spent several weeks on the Swedish charts, were written by Stig Anderson.

13 March Anni-Frid went to Germany for several days of promotion. Her producer, Olle Bergman, was keen to conquer the German market with the new single 'Härlig Är Vår Jord'. Unfortunately, this attempt ended in failure.

21 March The Hep Stars recorded two Benny and Björn songs: 'Speleman' (The Musician) and 'Precis Som Alla Andra' (Just Like All the Others).

1 April – 3 May The company of *The Charlie Norman Show* (Charlie Norman and his musicians, Anni-Frid Lyngstad and Hasse Burman) were at the Hamburger Börs in Stockholm. Among the songs and sketches included in the show was one in which Anni-Frid, Charlie Norman and Hasse Burman did a parody of the Supremes singing 'Bebbi-Läv'.

The day after the show's premiere, Göran Sellgren wrote in the daily newspaper *Dagens Nyheter*: 'Having become a real institution, this new show is quite entertaining. Its success owes a lot to the presence of Lennie Norman [Charlie's son] and Anni-Frid Lyngstad. Both of them have injected a new youthfulness into the show. Anni-Frid, who is just starting out as an artist, is pretty to look at and nice to listen to. However, the show would be perfect if Hasse Burman didn't pull so many faces and if Anni-Frid were to find a new dressmaker!'

Björn meets Agnetha

On 4 May 1969, Swedish Television recorded a documentary in Gothenburg and in Malmö paying homage to the Swedish composer Jules Sylvain. Among the guests were Agnetha Munther, Ingalill Nilsson, Sten Nilsson, Agnetha Fältskog and Björn Ulvaeus. Björn was on his own, performing the songs 'Tangokavaljeren' (The Tango Dancer) and 'Titta In I Min Lilla Kajuta' (Look In My Little Cabin). Long before the cameras started rolling, the two young singers had already become acquainted. Agnetha, who had admired the Hootenanny Singers' vocalist for a long time, went up to Björn and began, 'Hello, Björn, I've wanted to meet you for a long time. I really admire you!' Björn remembers the moment well: 'I recognized Agnetha immediately, as I'd seen her many times on television. I must admit that even if I didn't like the style of her songs, I found her seductive as a performer. I like her crystal-clear voice. We talked a lot, and I had the impression that we had known each other for a long time.' After the show, Björn and Agnetha began to see more of each other, and in August, they moved into a small studio flat in the Kungsholmen district of Stockholm, overlooking the Karlberg canal.

For the time being, the two young singers had to honour their respective professional engagements. Björn went on the road with the Hootenanny Singers and their new bassist, Lars Christian. Agnetha, for her part, began a summer tour with the singer Hans Smedberg and the eccentric Bertil Bertilsson. She does not have good memories of the summer of 1969: 'I was really fed up with shows. I couldn't stand being apart from Björn. Obviously, we phoned each other often, but that didn't make up for not having him with me.'

The couple tried to keep their relationship secret for as long as possible, but the news soon broke: the headline of one newspaper read 'Agnetha and Björn – the pop romance of the year', forcing the two young lovebirds to make their relationship public. Agnetha announced: 'I don't deny it – we are living together and we're very happy. My only regret is that we couldn't have kept our relationship hidden for longer.' Björn was more reserved with his announcement: 'We've been together for some time and we're in love. For the moment we don't want to make any plans. We are getting to know each other. Time will take care of the rest.' During the autumn, Björn and Agnetha left their tiny Kungsholmen studio flat for a three-roomed flat on Lilla Essingen island, close to the centre of Stockholm.

During the month of May, the Hep Stars decided to split up. Three of the musicians (the new guitarist Gus Horn, Lennart Hegland and Christer Pettersson) carried on under the name of the Rubber Band, with a more rock-style repertoire. Benny, together with singer Svenne Hedlund and his partner Charlotte Walker (better known as Lotta), would carry on with their cabaret tour. Before splitting up for good, the Hep Stars honoured their contract and toured the Swedish parks throughout the summer (this time without Björn, who was on tour with the Hootennany Singers).

Anni-Frid's life took a new turn. Supported by Benny, she now felt stronger and started building on her career, despite numerous criticisms in the press. Between 18 and 29 August, she was appearing again at the Hamburger Börs in Stockholm with *The Charlie Norman Show*. Anni-Frid and Benny were officially engaged on the opening night. This decision was savagely criticized by the daily newspaper *Aftonbladet*, who published a photo of Anni-Frid with Ragnar and their two children, declaring that the singer had intentionally destroyed her marriage to live a dream-like existence with Benny. The journalist added various details about the singer leaving for Stockholm, leaving her family behind, and so on. In response, Anni-Frid didn't mince her words: 'This is all complete fabrication. My divorce had been decided long before I met Benny. Ragnar and myself spent a long time talking before we decided to separate. In view of our situation, there was no other solution.'

31 August   The Hep Stars gave a farewell concert at Kungsträdgården in Stockholm in front of 25,000 people.

3 September   Agnetha appeared at the Aladdin club in Stockholm for one night only, together with her musicians and Bertil Bertilsson.

10 September   Anni-Frid recorded a new single: 'Peter Pan' and 'Du Betonar Kärlek Lite Fel' (You Pronounce the Word Love Badly). Benny produced the two songs and played piano on the tracks. 'Peter Pan' was written by Benny Andersson and Björn Ulvaeus. This was the first time that three future members of ABBA had worked on the same project.

12 September   Benny and Björn produced two songs for the Swedish singer Anna-Lena Löfgren.

25 September   Agnetha and Björn took part in the Grammisgalan 69 (Sweden's music-awards ceremony). Stig Anderson received the Best Songwriter Grammis for his song 'Gröna Små Äpplen' (Little Green Apples), recorded by Swedish jazz singer Monica Zetterlund.

2 October – 29 November   Charlie Norman, Anni-Frid, Hasse Burman and the rest of the company appeared at the Lisebergsteatern in Gothenburg. Maria Salomon wrote in the daily newspaper *Expressen*: 'Yes, Anni-Frid Lyngstad knows how to sing but she doesn't yet have a real stage presence.'

During October, Agnetha and Björn's work brought them together when the couple took part in a nightclub and discotheque tour called TOPP 69, intended to promote new talent from the Swedish charts. Also on the bill were Ola Håkansson, Nilsmen, Nina Lizell and Barbro Skinnar.

The month of November was quite busy for Björn and Benny. They were working on a new project: the writing and recording of music for a Swedish film called *Inga* II. Among the songs was 'Någonting Är På Väg' (Something's On Its Way), which would later feature on their *Lycka* (Happiness) album, and also the song 'She's My Kind of Girl'. Some of the recording sessions were carried over into December. The two musicians, along with Svenne Hedlund and his wife Lotta, were also signed up for a four-month tour of Sweden's main nightclubs, together with their musicians and the Danish comedian Finn Albert. For the whole of December, they performed at Valand in Gothenburg. The reviews were excellent. Göran Sellgren wrote in *Dagens Nyheter*: 'The artists work well as a group. Björn and Benny have got humour, personality and charm. The whole thing is fun, fresh and modern. I would have liked to have heard a bit more of Svenne and Lotta. But in view of the show's qualities, it's certain that there'll be a follow-up.'

From 3 December onwards, Anni-Frid appeared with the rest of the company of *The Charlie Norman Show* at the Berns music hall in Stockholm. Thorleif Hellbom wrote in *Dagens Nyheter*: 'The singers Anni-Frid Lyngstad and Laila Dahlin are not on their best form. This doesn't really work. Maybe it will during the course of the coming performances!' Despite the critics giving Anni-Frid and some other singers a rough ride, the show was a definite success. It stayed at this venue until the end of January before going on tour.

During this period, Stig Anderson and his partner Bengt Bernhag invited Björn and Benny to go into partnership with them to create the music-publishing company Union Songs AB. The Benny Andersson/Björn Ulvaeus partnership could now function on a full-time basis. After having had serious financial problems dogging him for many years due to the Hep Stars' debts, Benny felt the end was in sight. 'All my royalties went straight to the taxman,' he says. 'It took me four years to put right the errors of the past.'

Björn remembers: 'When I introduced Benny to Stig, he didn't think much of our future collaboration. He was finally convinced when he heard the first pieces that we had written together. From the start, we adopted quite an effective way of working. Benny would sit at the piano and I would pick up my guitar. Since we haven't ever been able to write or even read a single note of music, we would record our ideas on tape or play them to Stig in his office straight away.' The three men soon became a very prolific team. Once a melody had been decided upon, Stig would write the lyrics and get his two associates to record the song. By writing the words in English, he promised Björn and Benny an international career.

'BJÖRN WAS WARM AND TENDER. I LOOKED UP TO HIM. HE WAS WELL READ AND INTELLIGENT, VERY WELL INFORMED AND AT HOME WITH MOST THINGS. I WASN'T … HE HAD A CHARMING VOICE AND WAS AN ARTIST, LIKE ME. I FELT THAT WE WERE MARITALLY COMPATIBLE, WHICH IS QUITE APPARENT IN SOME OF THE PICTURES FROM THAT TIME!' AGNETHA

1970

Björn and Benny's nightclub tour with Svenne and Lotta was due to continue until March, and between 2 and 31 January, the four artists were appearing at the Hamburger Börs in Stockholm as well. They would then appear at the Arkaden in Malmö and tour several other towns. Björn and Benny were also working in the studio on new compositions and preparing demos for other artists, including two tracks for the Swedish singer Billy G-son.

21 January Agnetha recorded two new songs, 'Litet Solskensbarn' (Little Child of the Sun) and 'Om Tårar Vore Guld' (If Tears Were Made of Gold). The second song would be a massive hit in Sweden.

27 February Björn and Benny were in the studio with singer Billy G-son. They wrote and produced two songs for him: 'There's a Little Man' (Agnetha sang in the chorus) and 'I Saw It In the Mirror' (a later version of this track would feature on ABBA's *Ring Ring* album).

March saw the release of Björn and Benny's first single, 'She's My Kind of Girl' and 'Inga Theme'. The two songs were taken from the soundtrack to the film *Inga* II, which wouldn't be released until 30 October 1971.

6 March Anni-Frid recorded two new tracks at EMI studios: 'Där Du Går Lämnar Kärleken Spår' (Love Leaves Its Mark Wherever You Go) and 'Du Var Främling Här Igår' (You Were a Stranger Here Yesterday). Her previous recordings hadn't been as successful as expected, so her record company hesitated before allowing her to record an album. This would eventually take place in the autumn, with Benny producing. But for the time being, Anni-Frid carried on with her performances with *The Charlie Norman Show*, finally leaving the company at the end of June. As far as her single was concerned, *Helsingborgs Dagblad* wrote: 'With her tiny voice, Anni-Frid shares "Där Du Går Lämnar Kärleken Spår" with us, a song better known in English as "Love Grows". Anni-Frid sings a lovely Swedish version which ought to have as much success in this language as the English version. "Du Var Främling Här Igår" is a beautiful ballad which gives us a break from the torrid atmosphere of the A-side. These are two well-chosen songs.'

8 March Anni-Frid took part in a live television transmission lasting the entire evening entitled *Malmö – Stand By*, the proceeds of which would be given to charity for research into multiple sclerosis.

1 April Benny and Anni-Frid moved into a furnished studio flat in Vasastan in Stockholm. The first-floor flat was dark and so cramped that Benny couldn't move his piano in. He smiles when he remembers those days: 'We didn't have any choice, it was either the bed or the piano. For the first time since I was a child, I was living in a house without a piano. I was forced to practise at friends' houses or before concerts. I even played in a church, on a monumental organ. To pass the time, I listened to records a lot, but I really missed my keyboard. Nevertheless, despite these disadvantages, Frida and myself were very happy to be living together.'

A week later, Agnetha, Björn, Benny and Anni-Frid left Sweden for a few days' rest and sunshine in Cyprus. This trip marked the starting point of their future collaboration. 'We took along our guitars,' remembers Björn. 'And for the first time we realized that the girls' voices sounded perfect together. We immediately decided to include Agnetha and Frida in the recording of a future album, *Lycka* [Happiness].'

30 April Björn and Benny went back on tour with Svenne and Lotta, but this time they performed mainly in the country's *folkets parks*. They were accompanied by two Swiss musicians, bassist Gus Horn and drummer John Counz. The show mixed Swedish and English songs. Björn spoke to the audience and cracked jokes between songs. Anders Björkman wrote in

Lotta, Svenne, Benny & Björn on their nightclub tour

Expressen: 'This is a good family show. More spontaneous than last winter's tour. As soon as Björn begins a pot-pourri of his hits, you can hear all the young girls sighing. The jokes between the songs are amusing. To tell the truth, the whole show is straightforward and varied. Svenne, Lotta, Björn and Benny have clearly made progress!'

As for Anni-Frid, she was back on tour with Charlie Norman and his company. On 10 May, the singer made a significant return to the Svensktoppen when her single 'Där Du Går Lämnar Kärleken Spår' stayed at No. 8 for two weeks. A touch disillusioned, Anni-Frid declared in *Expressen*: 'The charts and me, that's a long story! I think I must hold the record for the greatest number of songs which have never made the charts … In three years, I've made eight records. Two of them have made the charts. The first one, "Härlig Är Vår Jord" spent a week in the hit parade. No longer than that.' Concerning the new song, Anni-Frid said: 'It won't stay in the charts for long. The public prefer songs with more melody. My style is too independent for the charts. But I like my records. And I think there's a quality about my songs.' Regarding her work with Charlie Norman, she said: 'We stay with him because we feel good with his company. But to tell the truth, I don't feel at ease on stage. I'm not sure of myself and I have stage fright. As a result, I become too static. I'll find a remedy for that in the future.'

16 May Agnetha gave the first concert of her summer tour in Karlshamn, in front of an audience of about 1000 people. She was accompanied on stage by singer-comedian Bert-Åke Varg and Rolf Carvenius's orchestra: Tommy Wåhlberg (guitar), Hans Johnsson (keyboard), Per-Arne Eklund (bass) and Birgitta Nordgren (drums). Among the songs that were best received by the audience were her new single 'Om Tårar Vore Guld' and a duet with Bert-Åke entitled 'Blommor Och Bin' (The Flowers and the Bees). Agnetha said of her partner: 'It's great to work with Bert-Åke, he's a real comedian. He knows how to work the audience.'

At the beginning of June, Björn and Benny began the studio recordings for *Lycka*. For several months, they had been preparing numerous demos. Not having found any musicians to perform them, they decided, in agreement with Stig, to work on an entire album on which they would sing together. Agnetha helped to write the song 'Liselott' and sang backing vocals with Anni-Frid on several songs. The ABBA musical 'family' gradually formed around the four young people, along with Sven-Olof Walldoff (conductor and arranger) and especially Michael B. Tretow, who would become Björn and Benny's sound engineer. Despite earlier professional concerns, Agnetha's optimism returned during her summer tour. Every time she started to sing her hit 'Om Tårar Vore Guld', the audience went wild. She told a journalist from *Aftonbladet*: 'It's fantastic, as soon as they play the first notes of the song, I can see people kissing each other in the audience.'

21–25 June Agnetha took a break from her tour. A recording session was arranged in a Parisian studio (probably for the French version of 'Om Tårar Vore Guld'), but curiously the session was cancelled at the last moment, and was replaced by a German-language recording session in Berlin.

'WE ASKED THE GIRLS TO HELP OUT WITH THE BACKING VOCALS FOR ONE OF THE RECORDS AND THAT WAS THE BIRTH OF THE WHOLE THING. PURE COINCIDENCE; I MEAN, WE COULD HAVE MET WITH TWO OFFICE GIRLS WHO COULDN'T SING AT ALL AND THEN THERE WOULDN'T HAVE BEEN ANY ABBA, I'M SURE.' **BJÖRN**

7 July Björn joined his friends Tony and Hansi (from the Hootenanny Singers) for a single concert given as part of the Västervik Song Festival, held in the ruins of Stegeholm Castle. Agnetha went along to support him.

25 July Agnetha and her company were singing in Gamleby. A few days later, Anders Björkman wrote in *Expressen*: 'The Agnetha Fältskog show is really going well, better than her show last year. However, there is one problem. When Agnetha and Bert-Åke Varg sing their duets "Blommor Och Bin" and "Inge Och Sten", everything goes perfectly. However when they perform their numerous solo numbers, it doesn't go so well. Why don't they stay together on stage for those numbers?'

29 August Agnetha ended her summer tour in Västerfärnebo, after forty-two concerts.

30 August Björn and Benny gave their last concerts with Svenne and Lotta in Bollnäs and Hudiksvall.

4 September On her return to Stockholm, Agnetha went into the studio to complete her third album, *Som Jag Är* (As I Am). Björn co-produced the record with Karl 'Little Gerhard' Lundkvist and performed a superb duet with Agnetha entitled 'Så Här Börjär Kärlek' (That's How Love Begins). The song very nearly didn't appear on the album because Stig Anderson usually refused to let any Polar Music artist feature on a rival label's record. He was against the release of the song as a single and Björn wasn't credited on the sleeve of Agnetha's album.

8 September Benny began producing Anni-Frid's first album at EMI studios. Among the songs recorded were several cover versions: 'Lycka' (by Björn and Benny), 'En Ton Av Tystnad' ('Sound of Silence' by Simon & Garfunkel) and 'En Lång Och Ödslig Väg' ('The Long and Winding Road' by the Beatles). 'At that time,' Frida says, 'you had to have several hit singles to your credit before you were able to record an entire album. That wasn't the case for me. In addition, my record company considered that I still hadn't found my style. They categorized me too much as a "jazz singer" and thought that I wasn't commercial enough. Benny let me tackle a repertoire which was more pop-based.'

Björn and Benny put the finishing touches to their *Lycka* album, due for release in the autumn. Although it received a lukewarm reception from the critics, the first single, 'Hej Gamle Man' (Hello Old Man), seemed to be popular with the radio programmers and the public. With Agnetha and Frida on backing vocals, 'Hej Gamle Man' can be considered to be the first song recorded by the future quartet.

29 September The two couples took part in the radio show *Våra Favoriter*. Agnetha sang 'Som Ett Eko' and Anni-Frid performed 'Barnen Sover', accompanied by Björn and Benny. The quartet also performed their new hit, 'Hej Gamle Man' and talked about the show they would be doing at the Trägårn nightclub in Gothenburg. Rehearsals would begin at the beginning of October.

4 October Anni-Frid, Benny and Stig attended Charlie Norman's fiftieth birthday party at his house in Bro.

Agnetha's third album, *Som Jag Är*, was released in October. It was accompanied by a single, 'Som Ett Eko' (Like an Echo). Göran Sellgren wrote in *Dagens Nyheter*: 'Agnetha Fältskog isn't too fussy as far as the choice of her singles is concerned – "Zigenarvän" proved that. And her new album *Som Jag Är* doesn't show any improvement. However, she doesn't sing too badly and the record is well arranged by Sven-Olof Walldoff.'

'I MUST HAVE SOME SORT OF RECORD IN FAILING TO GET INTO THE CHARTS.' **FRIDA**

'HOW CAN YOU CRITICIZE TWO COUPLES WHO HAD FALLEN IN LOVE AND WERE SINGING TOGETHER? THAT'S WHAT WE DID! IT WAS NOT A CONTROLLED IMAGE, IT WAS ABSOLUTELY NATURAL!' BJÖRN

'WE REALLY STARTED WORKING TOGETHER A LOT IN 1970 AND THE GIRLS BECAME INVOLVED AS WELL. I THINK BJÖRN AND I DECIDED THAT IT WAS STUPID FOR US TO SING WHEN WE HAD TWO SUCH GREAT SINGERS CLOSE TO US.' **BENNY**

1971

7 – 8 January Björn and Benny (accompanied by Agnetha and Anni-Frid) recorded 'Hej Musikant', the German-language version of 'Hej Gamle Man'. For the B-side, they chose 'Livet Går Sin Gång' (Life Goes At Its Own Pace), which became 'Was die Liebe Sagt' in German. The German lyrics were written by producer Hans Bradtke. The single was only released in Germany. The two musicians discovered that their song 'The Language of Love' (in Swedish, 'Livet Går Sin Gång') would soon be recorded by Françoise Hardy in both French and English.

In the middle of January, Anni-Frid and Benny completed the studio recordings for the album *Frida*. Prior to its launch, the record company EMI released a first single from the album, featuring the tracks 'Tre Kvart Från Nu' and 'En Liten Sång Om Kärlek' (A Little Song About Love). During this time, Agnetha and Björn spent two weeks on holiday in The Gambia.

26 January The two couples were among 225 guests at a massive party organized by Stig Anderson at his villa in Nacka, near Stockholm, for his birthday. Among the numerous gifts the producer received was a 10-metre-high flagpole!

20 February Björn and Benny celebrated an encouraging success overseas, when the English-language version of 'Livet Går Sin Gång' (The Language of Love) came sixth in the Malaga Song Festival. American singer Donna Hightower won first prize.

14 March Agnetha, Björn, Benny and Anni-Frid gave a concert in Hammarby, Stockholm, to mark the opening of the OK Biva-Huset service station.

31 March Frida's first album was released. The cover, designed by Ola Lager, had a gatefold sleeve. Although the photos inside the sleeve were excellent, the cover photo of Anni-Frid didn't do her justice. The album was praised by the critics. Hans Fridlund wrote in *Expressen*: 'I really don't know why Anni-Frid's records aren't more successful. She is one of our best singers, superior to all the other women in the charts. At least with Miss Lyngstad, she has personality and an unusual style.' *Dagens Nyheter*'s view was: 'It's time to take Anni-Frid Lyngstad seriously. It's a strong, perfect first album, gentle but still with lots of personality, humour, tenderness and even anger. When she sings, you realize that she's got something between her ears. Her style, which is quite simple, is unusually intelligent.' In *Folket*, Tommy Eriksson wrote: 'The *Frida* album is the perfect exclamation mark. A completely professional product with surprising precision. Not only does she have a voice full of great feeling but she is also sensual and expressive. She sings "Telegram För Fullmånen" so well that she really warms our hearts. It has everything: emotion, warmth and tenderness, which all adds up to make Anni-Frid a rare and intelligent artist.'

23 April Björn and Benny recorded a new single, 'Det Kan Ingen Doktor Hjälpa' (No Doctor Can Help That) and 'På Bröllop' (At the Wedding). Agnetha and Frida sang backing vocals.

30 April Agnetha, Björn and Benny began a tour of the parks which would last for several months (the first concerts were in Alingsås and Lidköping). The shows usually took place at the end of the week, leaving the three artists time to work on other projects. During a half-hour set, they performed about a dozen songs – their hits, of course, but also a cover of Graham Nash's 'Teach Your Children' and two comic sketches: 'Arga Unga Män' (Angry Young Men) by Bosse Carlgren and 'Koskenkorva' (the brand name of a Finnish vodka) by Lars Berghagen. They were accompanied on stage by Göran Lagerberg on bass and Kjell Jeppson on drums.

Hans Fridlund wrote in *Expressen*: 'It's a charming show from the trio Agnetha, Björn and Benny. They are good on stage and Björn and Agnetha seem very

loving as a couple. In total, there are ten songs which are very chart-oriented, although some of the songs are quite weak. Most memorable is a superb version of Graham Nash's "Teach Your Children" and two amusing sketches. Björn Ulvaeus still sings with a little nasal sound which is characteristic of him, whilst Miss Fältskog is still limited vocally. I'm sure that will change over the years …'. Bengt Melin, in *Aftonbladet*, wrote: 'The show is sincere, simple and very "hit parade". Agnetha Fältskog has more stage presence and sings more in tune now. Björn Ulvaeus got lots of applause for "Hej Gamle Man" and for his duets. As for Benny Andersson, he's a real stage animal these days. But it looks like they've gone for the easy option. It's a shame they don't put more into different songs. Benny is one of our rare real composers.'

13 May Agnetha went back into the Metronome studios to begin recording her fourth album *När En Vacker Tanke Blir En Sång* (When a Beautiful Idea Becomes a Song). Björn helped to write some of the songs and produced the entire record.

25 May The two couples were together again in the Europa Film studios for the recording of Lill-Babs's single 'Välkommen Till Världen' (Welcome To the World). The song, composed by Björn and Benny, had been rejected by the Swedish Eurovision-selection jury. The two musicians produced the record, provided some of the musical parts and, together with Agnetha and Frida, sang backing vocals.

At the beginning of June, Anni-Frid went to Malta with singer Lars (Lasse) Berghagen to rehearse for their summer tour of the Swedish parks. Lars and Frida recorded two duets which were released as a single on the Polydor label, 'En Kväll Om Sommaren' (A Summer's Evening) and 'Vi Vet Allt Men Nästan Inget' (We Know Everything But Almost Nothing).

15 June Agnetha, Björn and Benny sang on the television programme *Midsommardans Från Solliden* on Sweden's TV2. This programme, recorded at Skansen park in Stockholm, brought together a host of stars including Lill-Babs, Brita Borg and the conductor Sven-Olof Walldoff. Among other songs, Agnetha sang the two tracks from her new single, 'Kungens Vaktparad' (The Parade of the Royal Guard) and 'Jag Vill Att Du Ska Bli Lycklig' (I Want You To Be Happy).

6 July Björn and Agnetha were married in the little church of Verum, a parish of Skåne in southern Sweden. The couple tried to keep the ceremony secret, but more than 3000 people invaded the village to witness the wedding of the year. Agnetha arrived in a horse-drawn carriage, and when she made her entrance into church, Mendelssohn's 'Wedding March' rang out, followed by 'Wedding', an old Hep Stars song, played on the organ by Benny. Björn recalls: 'When I contacted the minister Uno Wardener, he asked me what our profession was and he thought I said "atheist" instead of "artist". Shocked, he replied that he wouldn't be able to carry out the service!'

Anni-Frid with Lars Berghagen & his musicians, Bo Dahlman, Lasse Svensson & Lukas Lindholm

When they came out of the church, the crowd surged forward. The couple fought their way through to the waiting carriage and Agnetha had her foot trodden on by one of the horses. The ceremony was followed by a dinner at the Wittsjö inn for thirty-nine guests and Ada, the newlyweds' black bulldog. On the menu were smoked eel, tournedos and Arctic berry ice-cream.

'Björn and I found this church when we were on tour,' remembers Agnetha. 'I'd always dreamed of getting married in a little white church. I must say that I was overjoyed, the ceremony was definitely one of the best days of my life. After the service, part of the crowd followed us to the inn shouting "We want to see the newlyweds!" Björn and myself were forced to appear on the first-floor balcony. We were treated like a royal couple.' There was to be no honeymoon, as Agnetha and Björn were due back on tour four days later.

'WE WANTED A FAMILY AND PLANNED CHILDREN FROM THE START, BUT NO BABY CAME ALONG. I BEGAN TO GO FOR TESTS. EVERY MONTH I WAS DISAPPOINTED WHEN NOTHING HAPPENED. WE EVEN THOUGHT ABOUT ADOPTION … WHEN I EVENTUALLY BECAME PREGNANT, I COULD HARDLY BELIEVE IT… I RANG BJÖRN AND YELLED DOWN THE PHONE, "WE'RE GOING TO HAVE A BABY!" HE WAS OVERJOYED AND CAME STRAIGHT HOME WITH A BOTTLE OF CHAMPAGNE.' **AGNETHA**

Linköping Folkets Park

The day after the ceremony, Stig received a telephone call from Stockholm informing him of the suicide of his friend and associate Bengt Bernhag, who had been one of the founders of Polar Music. Bengt had discovered the Hootenanny Singers and had personally taken care of their career. He had suffered serious health problems during the past year and had turned down the invitation to the wedding of his protégé, thinking that he was too physically run-down. Björn, who had thought of him as a second father, was profoundly affected by his death. 'I owe him so much,' he explained. 'He taught me the ropes of this profession. Still shocked by this terrible news, Stig asked me to go out with him for a boat trip on the lake next to the inn. He wanted to ask me discreetly to take over from Bengt at Polar Music. I accepted on the sole condition that Benny would also be part of our collaboration. Stig accepted but offered just one salary between us.'

12 July Anni-Frid recorded two new songs for her next single, 'Min Egen Stad' (My Home Town) and 'En Gång Är Ingen Gång' (Once Is Not At All).

15 July Benny and Björn recorded some new demos with a view to making a second album as a duo. A single was released the following month, including 'Tänk Om Jorden Vore Ung' (Just Think If the World Was Young), with Agnetha and Frida on backing vocals, from the *Lycka* album and a new song, 'Träskofolket' (People In Clogs). This song was inspired by 'Utvandrarna' (The Emigrants), a classic book by Swedish writer Vilhelm Moberg in which he relates that in the nineteenth century, Americans nicknamed the Swedes who had emigrated to the United States 'the people in clogs'. Despite the fact that some other songs were completed during the following months, for some reason, Björn and Benny's second album would never see the light of day.

From now on, the two men would be full-time producers at the heart of Polar Music. Their first production was a compilation album for the Hootenanny Singers entitled *Våra Vackraste Visor* (Our Most Beautiful Songs). They then produced an album entitled *Lena* for Swedish singer Lena Andersson, and the first record for Polar Music's promising new artist, Ted Gärdestad. Stig remembered: 'We auditioned Ted and his brother Kenneth two years previously. They had a lot of talent but were too young to start a singing career.

When Ted came back to see us again, Björn and Benny immediately wanted to work with him. His first album worked really well and he was even the subject of a TV documentary.'

8 August Anni-Frid and Lars Berghagen reached No. 8 in the Svensktoppen with 'En Kväll Om Sommaren'. Their tour of the Swedish parks ended on 28 August. Hans Fridlund wrote in *Expressen*: 'It's saying a lot to describe it as a real show. The ensemble enter the stage from the left and go off in the same direction 35 minutes later. In that time they give us eight songs and two very bad monologues, written by Lena Hansson … But thanks go to Miss Lyngstad, who is an exceptional singer!'

28 August Agnetha, Björn and Benny ended their summer tour with two concerts in Eskilstuna and Köping.

During the month of September, Björn and Benny dedicated their time to writing and recording new songs for Lena Andersson and Ted Gärdestad. Agnetha and Anni-Frid sang backing vocals on a number of the songs.

22 October Anni-Frid made her début at the Folkan Theatre, Stockholm, in a variety show called *Mina Favoriter*. The show, devised by entertainer Kar de Mumma, was produced by Hasse Ekman. He brought together a host of stars including Siw Malmkvist, Siv Ericks, Lars Berghagen, Stig Järrel and Rolf

Bengtson. Anni-Frid performed three songs in the show, including a duet with Lars Berghagen, 'Vem Släcker Månen' (Who Turns Out the Moon) and another with singer Siv Ericks. *Mina Favoriter* ran for seven months.

Anni-Frid's single 'Min Egen Stad' went straight into the Svensktoppen at No. 3. The song, which stayed in the charts for six weeks, reached No. 1 on 7 November. It was her first real hit, and EMI decided to issue a new pressing of the *Frida* album featuring 'Min Egen Stad'.

During the autumn, Benny, Björn and Anni-Frid finished the recording of Agnetha's fourth album, *När En Vacker Tanke Blir En Sång*. Its release was planned for the end of November.

30 October   The film N*ågon Att Älska* (Someone To Love) – formerly titled
I*nga* II – was released, with music by Björn Ulvaeus and Benny Andersson.
Filmed in Sweden by the American director Joseph W. Sarno, with Tommy
Blom in the main role, the full-length feature lacked a plot and was a
resounding flop.

3 December   Polar Music released the Hootenanny Singers compilation
album. To mark the occasion, Swedish Television screened a 35-minute
programme entitled V*isunderhållning* (Entertainment By Song). The Hootenanny
Singers, accompanied by Benny on accordion, were interviewed and
performed six new songs.

At that time, Anni-Frid was touring the Swedish parks with Roffe Berg. Her contract with EMI having expired, she naturally signed to the Polar Music label, for whom she recorded two new songs, 'Man Vill Ju Leva Lite Dessemellan' (You Still Want To Live a Bit In Between) and 'Ska Man Skratta Eller Gråta' (Should We Laugh Or Cry). The single was produced by Björn and Benny, who also sang on the backing vocals together with Agnetha.

26 August Agnetha's summer tour ended with two concerts in Örebro and Vretstorp.

The Japanese record company were looking for a follow-up to the hit 'She's My Kind of Girl'. There was even talk of a special album for the Japanese market. Nevertheless, Björn and Benny had some difficulties with their Japanese representatives, who thought their lyrics were not commercial enough. After 'Santa Rosa' was rejected, the song 'Love Has Its Ways', written by Koichi Morita, was submitted to the two musicians. After some negotiation, the single was released with a new track entitled 'Rock 'n' Roll Band' on the B-side.

With December approaching, Stig was planning to release a record of the most popular Christmas tunes in Sweden. He asked Björn and Benny to produce *När Juldagsmorgon Glimmar* (When Christmas Morning Is Shining), an album bringing together all of Polar Music's artists (including Lena Andersson, Svenne Hedlund and Arne Lamberth). Agnetha was not available, due to her contract with CBS-Cupol. Frida chose to sing her two favourite songs, 'När Det Lider Mot Jul' (When Christmas Is Coming) and 'Gläns Över Sjö Och Strand' (It's Shining Over the Lake and the Shore). Two tracks by the Hootenanny Singers were also featured on the album: 'Nu Tändas Tusen Juleljus' (A Thousand Christmas Candles Are Being Lit) and 'Gå Sion, Din Konung Att Möta' (Go Sion, To Meet Your King).

Then, for the second time in her career, Anni-Frid hit No. 1 on the Swedish hit parade. This time, it was the song 'Man Vill Ju Leva Lite Dessemellan' which had taken her to the top of the charts. The song, which entered the Swedish charts on 17 September, was a cover version of the Italian song 'Chia Salta Il Fosso'.

18 September Agnetha recorded a new single which was produced by Björn, 'Tio Mil Kvar Till Korpilombolo' (Ten Miles More To Korpilombolo) and 'Så Glad Som Dina Ögon' (As Happy As Your Eyes). The record entered the Swedish charts on 10 December and reached No. 5.

8 October EMI, hoping to benefit from Anni-Frid's recent success, released a compilation album featuring a selection of her best Swedish songs from the period 1967–71.

10 October The single 'People Need Love' was released in France and Belgium on the Vogue label, thanks to Alain Boublil, one of the first to sign a contract with Stig Anderson. Alain recounts: 'I had created Baboo, my own music production and publishing company. One day Stig, who was a very good friend, brought me 'People Need Love'. That's how it all started. We signed the contract and the disc was distributed by Vogue.'

21 October Björn and Benny were working again with Ted Gärdestad, who was recording his second album, *Ted*, in the Metronome studios. By now, the project for Björn and Benny's second album as a duo had definitely been abandoned. After the success of 'People Need Love', Stig reckoned that from now on the quartet could envisage a career beyond Scandinavia. He persuaded the four of them to do an album in English, with Agnetha and Anni-Frid doing most of the singing. Among the first tracks to be recorded were 'Nina, Pretty Ballerina' and 'He Is Your Brother'.

In the middle of November, Björn, Benny, Agnetha and Frida flew to Japan, where their single 'She's My Kind of Girl' had sold more than 500,000 copies. The two couples were welcomed as superstars. CBS Japan took advantage of the visit to release the single 'Love Has Its Ways'.

At the same time, Polar Music released the quartet's second single in Scandinavia, featuring 'He Is Your Brother', with 'Santa Rosa' on the B-side.

On their return to Stockholm, as the group were busy preparing the new album, some good news arrived from the National Television Society. The quartet were invited to put forward a song for selection for the Eurovision Song Contest. Stig, Benny and Björn saw it as an excellent opportunity to reach a larger public. The three men quickly set to work, deciding to compose the song in the calm environment of the island of Viggsö, in the Swedish archipelago, where Björn and Agnetha, Benny and Frida, and Stig and Gudrun all owned chalets. Benny said: 'Out there, you can really get stuck into things. No unwanted telephone calls, no recording studios, nothing. We just write and eat and down the odd beer – or something a bit stronger.' Stig added: 'We usually write a great deal at Christmas and New Year. And once we really get started, it doesn't matter what time of the day or night it is. If we've been working all night, we can sleep all day instead. Nobody comes to disturb us.'

Agnetha's pregnancy was closely documented by the women's press. At the beginning of December, *Vecko-Revyn* magazine chose to put the group on the front of their Christmas issue. The two couples were photographed in a Christmas Eve dinner setting, in Agnetha and Björn's flat. The coverline was: 'At home with Björn Ulvaeus and Agnetha Fältskog: their last Christmas without a child.'

Frida & Agnetha during the *Vecko-Revyn* Christmas photo session

Agnetha, Björn & Linda praising the merits of Semper baby foods

23 February Agnetha gave birth to a baby girl, who was named Linda Elin. A few days later, Björn allowed journalists and photographers into the Danderyd hospital room for a press conference with mother and baby at his side. Both were in excellent health, with the baby weighing 3.1 kilograms and measuring 51 centimetres. Agnetha returned home on 29 February.

Stig Anderson, encouraged by the success of 'Ring Ring', was eager to promote the record outside the borders of Scandinavia. The foreign release of the single would be supported by a promotional tour of several northern European countries. Polar Music announced to the press that the album would be released at the end of March. In the middle of March, the group recorded the last three tracks: 'Disillusion', 'Love Isn't Easy (But It Sure Is Hard Enough)' and 'I Saw It In the Mirror'. 'Disillusion' had originally been a Swedish track entitled 'Mina Ögon' (My Eyes), composed by Agnetha and later appearing on her solo album.

'IN ONE WAY IT WAS QUITE AN ADVANTAGE HAVING TO WAIT ANOTHER YEAR BEFORE WINNING, BECAUSE IN THE MEANTIME WE LEARNED QUITE A LOT ABOUT HOW THINGS WORKED IN OTHER COUNTRIES. LATER ON, WHEN WE WON THE CONTEST WITH "WATERLOO", THE ORGANIZATIONAL SIDE OF THINGS WORKED EXTREMELY WELL. WE WERE PREPARED IN A COMPLETELY DIFFERENT WAY.' **BJÖRN** ON EUROVISION

For some time, the two couples had been faced with numerous problems concerning the name of the group. Obviously Björn, Benny, Agnetha and Anni-Frid was too long, too difficult to pronounce and too hard to remember. 'In private,' explained Stig, 'I'd got into the habit of calling them ABBA, because of their initials. I liked the name, but to be honest, we hadn't gone to any great lengths to try to find another name. With the assistance of the newspaper *Göteborgs-Tidningen*, we ran a competition to find a name for our group. The results were surprising and we had suggestions as varied as Flower Power, Black Devils, Golden Diamonds, Baba, and strange as it may seem, 80 per cent of people chose ABBA. How could we reject a name which we liked and which was short, international and easy to remember? The only problem was that Abba is the name of the largest brand of canned herring in Sweden. Nevertheless, I was determined to keep this name, even though we were left open to all kinds of jokes. I made a point of phoning Anders Ekström, managing director of the company which produces this famous Swedish product, and he very kindly allowed us to use the name "Abba" on one condition: that the group wouldn't discredit his company. He confessed that he couldn't have dreamed of better publicity for his product!'

At the beginning of August, ABBA went to Oslo to perform 'Ring Ring' on the TV show M*omarkedet*. All the profits from this famous Norwegian programme went to the Red Cross.

13 August   A big night for Polar Music. Stig had invited numerous people to celebrate several different events: the tenth anniversary of the record company, the tenth anniversary of the Hootenanny Singers, and also to present awards to the artists on the label. Agnetha, Björn, Benny and Anni-Frid were presented with a gold disc for sales of the Swedish and English versions of the 'Ring Ring' single, as well as a diamond disc for the 'Ring Ring' album. Members of the Hootenanny Singers received gold discs for sales of their albums *Våra Vackraste Visor* 2 and *Dan Andersson På Vårt Sätt*, and Ted Gärdestad received a gold disc for his album *Ted*. To mark the event, Polar Music released a retrospective album commemorating ten years of the record company.

The defeat of 'Ring Ring' in the Melodifestivalen was in many ways a beneficial experience for Björn, Benny and Stig. The next year, the jury of experts would be replaced by a panel made up of a cross-section of people from different regions of Sweden. The three men were determined to go all out to win the 1974 Eurovision Song Contest, and with Stig's professionalism, it was clear that not even the tiniest detail would be overlooked.

From September until the end of the year, the three men composed, wrote and recorded at the Metronome studios, working on the tracks which would feature on the group's second album, scheduled for release in the spring of 1974. The first songs were 'Dance (While the Music Still Goes On)', which is reminiscent of Phil Spector, 'Suzy-Hang-Around', one of the few songs sung by Benny, 'My Mama Said', 'Honey Honey' (of which a Swedish-language version would later be recorded), 'What About Livingstone', 'King Kong Song' and the excellent ballad 'Gonna Sing You My Lovesong', sung by Frida.

11 October   Vogue released the single 'Nina, Pretty Ballerina', with 'He Is Your Brother' on the B-side. The 'Ring Ring' single had flopped in France; Alain Boublil's team had underestimated the song's potential.

12 October   'Ring Ring' was released in Britain, much later than in other countries. Stig had had the single refused by three record companies (EMI, Decca and PYE), and it was only after long negotiations that he finally managed to sign a contract with Epic/CBS. Due to the lack of promotion, the single wasn't a hit. However, Irish group the Others managed to get into the Top 20 with their version of the song.

18 November   The Hootenanny Singers' song 'Omkring Tiggaren Från Luossa' (Around the Beggar From Luossa) broke a Svensktoppen record, having been in the chart for fifty-two weeks. At the same time, the Polar Music team learned that 'I Am Just a Girl' had entered the Japanese charts.

'I THINK THE REASON THAT BJÖRN AND I WORK SO WELL TOGETHER IS THAT WE COMPLEMENT EACH OTHER'
BENNY

Completely absorbed by the group's activities and especially by her daughter Linda, Agnetha was now recording less and less as a solo artist. During the autumn, CBS-Cupol released a compilation album, *Bästa* (Best of), and a single from it, 'En Sång Om Sorg Och Glädje' (A Song About Sorrow and Joy). This was the first track produced by Agnetha. It climbed to the top of the Svensktoppen chart over six consecutive weeks. The lyrics were written by Stig Anderson.

After having officially announced ABBA's participation in the forthcoming Melodifestivalen, Stig brought his team together to present the results of his recent enquiries, having sounded out the opinions of numerous European showbusiness professionals as to what kind of song ABBA should select for the contest. It seemed that a rhythmic song which was more pop-oriented would be successful with the Eurovision jury. The public were tired of sugary-sweet ballads. Stig was convinced that they had to present a short, catchy song which could be understood in every language. During the course of this meeting, he also told the group about his ideas regarding their conquest of the European market.

Björn and Benny had never been so prolific as they were towards the end of 1973, putting the finishing touches to all the songs for the forthcoming album and completing even more songs than necessary. Among these demos, Stig found two tracks which interested him. He made the most of a trip to the Canary Islands – away from the telephone and professional obligations – to take the tapes away and set to work. 'I was very inspired by these melodies,' he explained. 'My first idea was a name I'd found in a cookery book, "Honey Pie", but I had trouble developing lyrics around this title. Finally, after searching through an encyclopedia, I found "Waterloo". As for the second track, while I was on holiday in Las Palmas, I often heard people say "*Hasta mañana*" on the radio and in the street. I liked this expression and thought it fitted the music perfectly. The text came together very quickly.'

17 December The whole team were in the Metronome studios for the recording of 'Waterloo' and another track, 'Watch Out'. The following day, they recorded 'Sitting In the Palmtree' and 'Hasta Mañana'.

It was now time to choose the song which ABBA would take to the Melodifestivalen the following February. After having played the songs for the group's entourage, 'Waterloo' was finally chosen. There were several reasons for this decision, but the most important factor was that the song was sung by the whole group, whereas 'Hasta Mañana' has only one vocalist, Agnetha. The rhythm and energy of 'Waterloo' were also deciding factors. 'I remember that they asked me which song I thought they should choose,' says guitarist Janne Schaffer, 'and I told them that they were fools if they didn't go for "Waterloo".' (T*he Complete Recording Sessions*, 1994.)

☆ ☆ ☆ ☆

Agnetha, Björn, Benny and Anni-Frid toured the Swedish parks from 15 June (Gothenburg) until 9 September (Malmö). In order that the tour should not interfere with their studio work or Björn and Agnetha's family life, the group chose to perform only at weekends. Accompanied by three musicians, the two couples gave their audiences a 30-minute show. The star attraction was a song sung by Benny, accompanying himself on the ukulele.

The show received mixed reviews. Anders Björkman wrote in *Expressen*: 'This monotonous show follows on from their chart successes. The girls dance and the boys play their instruments. Only Benny manages to lift the show from the depths of lethargy with his song. The rest of the show is mechanical.' On the other hand, the *Göteborgs-Posten* wrote: 'Throughout the entire show, you can see how pleased the group are to be giving their audience a show of quality. They work well together, with a fast tempo and an interesting style.'

Anni-Frid explains: 'There are happy memories of this tour, but it was time for it to come to an end because we were all exhausted. I lost 7 kilos. When you realize that sometimes we even did three shows on the same day, it was madness!'

JUNE

Friday	15	Gothenburg (Liseberg Park)	
Saturday	16	Rättvik	21.00
Saturday	16	Avesta	24.00
Sunday	17	Högsjö	16.00
Sunday	17	Årjäng	21.00
Sunday	17	Åmotfors	23.00
Friday	22	Lappvattnet	22.00
Friday	22	Lycksele	01.00
Saturday	23	Överkalix	21.30
Saturday	23	Tärendö	24.00
Saturday	30	Östervåla	22.00
Saturday	30	Gävle	24.00

JULY

Sunday	01	Söderbykarl	17.00
Sunday	01	Stockholm (Kungsträdgården)	19.30
Wednesday	04	Gamleby	
Thursday	05	Simonstorp	22.00
Friday	06	Oskarshamn	23.00
Saturday	07	Södertälje	22.00
Saturday	07	Mariefred	23.30
Sunday	08	Grängesberg	19.30
Sunday	08	Dala-Floda	22.00
Friday	13	Köping	
Saturday	14	Säter	21.30
Saturday	14	Borlänge	23.30
Sunday	15	Mora	23.00
Friday	20	Sunnemo	23.00
Saturday	21	Lysvik	21.30
Saturday	21	Sysslebäck	24.00
Sunday	22	Kungsbacka	18.00
Sunday	22	Vegby	21.00
Friday	27	Viskan	
Friday	27	Hammarstrand	
Saturday	28	Noraström	21.30
Sunday	29	Svenstavik	

AUGUST

Friday	03	Alstermo	21.00
Friday	03	Kalmar	23.30
Saturday	04	Mariestad	21.15
Saturday	04	Falköping	23.30
Sunday	05	Lerdala	16.30
Sunday	05	Trädet	19.00
Saturday	11	Kiruna	
Sunday	12	Skellefteå	
Tuesday	14	Söderhamn	21.00
Wednesday	15	Östersund: Jamtli	19.30
Friday	17	Nykroppa	22.30
Saturday	18	Hofors	
Monday	20	Stockholm (Malmen Club)	24.00
Friday	24	Österbybruk	22.30
Saturday	25	Örebro	21.30
Saturday	25	Kristinehamn	24.00
Sunday	26	Karlstad	15.00
Friday	31	Mysen (Norway)	

SEPTEMBER

Saturday	01	Karlskoga	21.00
Saturday	01	Vretstorp	23.00
Sunday	02	Göteborg (LOBO restaurant)	
Friday	07	Sölvesborg	20.30
Saturday	08	Kristianstad	21.00
Sunday	09	Malmö	20.00

'MOST OF THE SONGS IN THE CONTEST WERE BOOMPA-BOOMPA. WE DECIDED TO WRITE SOMETHING THAT WAS MORE OF A POP SONG AND WHICH WOULD CHANGE THE EUROVISION SONG CONTEST SITUATION.' **STIG**

1974

The new year began with the recording of the Swedish-language version of 'Honey Honey' at the Metronome Studios and some extra sessions to finish off the recording of 'Waterloo'.

Stig's party at his villa in Nacka after the Melodifestivalen

9 February As in previous years, Swedish Television would screen the Melodifestivalen live. Agnetha, Björn, Benny and Anni-Frid were confident. Their performance of 'Waterloo' in Swedish was excellent and their conductor Sven-Olof Walldoff caused a sensation in his Napoleon costume. When presenter Johan Sandström announced the winners who would be going on to compete in Brighton, the result surpassed all expectations: ABBA had come first, with an overwhelming victory of 302 points against 211 points for Lars Berghagen and his song 'Min Kärlekssång Till Dig' (My Love Song To You). *Aftonbladet* announced: 'The voice of the people – the best song has won at last!'

The evening came to a close with a massive party organized by Stig at his villa in Nacka. Surrounded by all their friends and colleagues, the four group members relived the events of the evening with a video borrowed from Swedish Television. For fun, Stig also offered his guests some *Napoleon bakelse* (Napoleon cake).

10 February Prior to the Eurovision Song Contest, Stig had put together a promotional strategy to ensure that whether or not they were victorious in Brighton, the single would be released simultaneously in every European country. Over five days, he had visited the record companies and music publishers of Copenhagen, Hamburg, Vienna, Amsterdam, London, Brussels and Paris. In his briefcase was an English-language version of 'Waterloo', a press release and a biography of the group in four languages. 'By doing this I was reinforcing our presence in the contest,' explained Stig. 'I didn't want to miss even the tiniest detail because this event is a superb springboard for singers who want to reach an audience outside their own country. It also gives you the opportunity to compete with international artists. In the United States, I even paid for advertising pages in the monthly publications *Billboard* and *Cashbox* to promote the song.'

21 February Benny began work on *Frida Ensam*, Anni-Frid's second solo album.

With the recording of the *Waterloo* album complete, photographer Ola Lager organized a photo shoot to illustrate the sleeve. This took place in the magnificent setting of Gripsholm Castle, near Mariefred, about 50 kilometres west of Stockholm. It was bassist Mike Watson who wore the Napoleon uniform in the photos.

During March, Björn and Benny finished recording Ted Gärdestad's *Upptåg* (Practical Joke) album. Agnetha and Frida sang backing vocals on some of the tracks.

4 March Polar Music released the *Waterloo* album in Sweden, and the singles of the same title in Swedish and English. After just four weeks, the group had sold 125,000 copies of the album and 85,000 copies of the singles.

Hans Fridlund, always harsh, wrote in *Expressen*: 'It's obvious that this album is going to achieve monstrous sales. The Swedes, in voting for ABBA and their song "Waterloo", made the right decision. Björn and Benny have analysed current pop trends well but also remember the sounds of the past. "Honey Honey" and "Suzy-Hang-Around" are a bit reminiscent of the Beach Boys (although ABBA don't sing quite as well).

'WE WERE YOUNG, EXTREMELY AMBITIOUS AND SELF-CONFIDENT AT THE SAME TIME. AND ALL THAT PLAYED A PART. THAT'S THE SORT OF THING THAT YOU ONLY DO ONCE IN YOUR LIFETIME.' BJÖRN

'While "Watch Out" is a clumsy attempt at soul, "Gonna Sing You My Lovesong" is a bluesy ballad in the Leon Russel gospel style. "Sitting In the Palmtree" has Caribbean-reggae influences and "Hasta Mañana" leans towards the German *schlager* sound. One shouldn't complain about these changes. And all those who previously thought of ABBA as a sugary-sweet band will find quite a few songs here which really move because of Janne Schaffer's guitar. But do Björn and Benny really have to mix all these different styles on the same record? They're obviously clever. But as far as I'm concerned, I much prefer it when I can feel the real personality of the musicians rather than listening to this outpouring of abilities. I would also like Benny Andersson to use less piano-moog on the musical backing.'

7 March   The 'Waterloo' single had a quiet release on the Vogue label in France and Belgium. After the Brighton victory, a new edition would be released with the caption '1er Grand Prix Eurovision 1974'.

15 March   The group recorded the German-language version of 'Waterloo', written by Gerd Müller-Schwanke. Polydor Germany released the single on 5 April.

27 March   Frida returned to the KMH studio to record two new songs, 'Chapel of Love' and 'That's When the Music Takes Me'. Unfortunately, neither of these tracks was included on the *Frida Ensam* album.

28 March   Agnetha recorded a new solo single, featuring 'Golliwog' and 'Came For Your Love'. The first track would feature on her forthcoming album, but in a Swedish-language version entitled 'Gulleplutt'.

1 April   ABBA, their musicians, Stig and the whole entourage left for London. In the British capital, the group met journalists at a press conference organized by music-publishing company United Artists. It was a chance for Agnetha, Björn, Benny and Anni-Frid to test the water before the Eurovision Song Contest. The response was quite warm, with comments such as 'You've got a good song!'. Two days later, ABBA left London and travelled to Brighton.

5 April   Epic released the 'Waterloo' single in Britain. The following evening saw the famous victory (see the next chapter, 'Brighton Fever').

8 April   The group left Brighton for London. En *route*, Agnetha, Björn, Benny and Anni-Frid had the opportunity to bask in their victory when they heard 'Waterloo' on the radio. A second surprise was the announcement by the DJ that 15,000 copies had been sold within two hours that morning.

A champagne reception awaited them at the Grosvenor House hotel. During their stay in London, the two couples tried to give themselves some time to do a little shopping, despite their hectic timetable of press conferences, radio interviews, photo sessions in Hyde Park and at Waterloo station (for the *Daily Express*) and a reception with the Swedish ambassador to Britain, Ole Jödahl, who congratulated them on their performance. Agnetha, who was suffering from acute tonsillitis and a temperature, only managed to keep going due to medication.

10 April   ABBA performed on *Top of the Pops*, Britain's most popular TV pop-music programme, watched by 14 million viewers. The impact of their performance was so great that a week afterwards, 'Waterloo' went from No. 17 to No. 2 in the charts.

11 April   The members of the group flew to Hamburg and recorded an Easter show for German television, surrounded by rabbits and chicks. Just before midnight, they landed back at Stockholm's Arlanda airport. 'Our arrival was very quiet because we weren't expected until the following day,'

Performing 'Waterloo' on the TV show *Domino*, Paris

remembers Benny. 'We couldn't wait to get back home. After all the stress and strain we needed to rest. Anni-Frid and myself went straight back home to Vallentuna, a suburb of Stockholm. At last we could have some peace and quiet. We opened a bottle of champagne and reminisced about our trip to England.'

During the Easter weekend, Agnetha, Björn, Benny and Anni-Frid, together with their close friends, went to the island of Viggsö to relax before launching into promoting 'Waterloo'. 'When we were in Brighton, surrounded by journalists, we often dreamed of this moment,' said Benny. 'For the first time in ages we were free again. It was also the chance to review things with Stig and to think about future engagements. It was in fact at this moment that we made the decision for cancel the summer tour of the Swedish parks.'

16 April Stig sent an apologetic letter to the directors of the thirty parks where the group had planned to perform. The press reacted with headlines such as: 'ABBA no longer need Sweden because they are now going to conquer the whole world.' Stig and Björn responded with a statement: 'We are very proud to represent Sweden overseas. From now on, we have to guarantee that the group is promoted in all four corners of the world. Refusing to do television in New York or Madrid would be a big mistake. In addition, we are preparing ABBA's next album and have to spend time producing other artists at Polar Music, for instance Ted Gärdestad and Lena Andersson. If we go on tour, we have to allow a month for preparation and rehearsals as well as a month on the road. We don't want to exhaust ourselves! Nevertheless, we are planning a tour of Europe and Sweden at the end of the year. No contract had been signed with the parks, it was only a verbal agreement.'

17 April After this short break in Sweden, Agnetha, Björn, Benny and Anni-Frid flew to Paris. Unfortunately, they had little time to explore the capital, as their schedule was so tight. In three days, they took part in the radio programme RTL *Non Stop* (presented by Jacques Martin), and the TV shows *Midi-Première* (presented by Danièle Gilbert) and Guy Lux's *Domino*. Photo

shoots and even a recording session at the Vogue studio for the French-language version of 'Waterloo' took place. The track was produced by Claude-Michel Schönberg and Alain Boublil (who wrote the French text); this was the partnership that went on to write the musical *Les Misérables*. The single was released on 10 May in limited quantities. For the B-side, Vogue chose 'Gonna Sing You My Lovesong'.

22 April The group returned to Stockholm to attend the annual *Expressen* party at the Operakällaren restaurant. Every major artist and media personality was invited.

24 April ABBA recorded *The Eddy Becker Show* for Dutch television. In England, their success was so great and demand for them so high that the BBC decided to buy and televise the Dutch recording. ABBA continued promotion with a visit to Germany where they appeared on *The Peter Frankenfeld Show*.

On the same day, *Expressen* printed the first details of ABBA's chart successes in Europe. Two weeks after the Brighton victory, 'Waterloo' was already No. 2 in England (it would reach No. 1 on 4 May), No. 3 in Austria, No. 1 in Germany, No. 1 in Belgium, No. 3 in Holland, No. 13 in France, No. 23 in Italy, No. 1 in Norway, No. 1 in Sweden and No. 3 in Denmark.

2 May Vogue released the *Waterloo* album in France and Belgium. In France, the single made great progress (No. 3 on the RTL chart), but this did not help to boost sales of the album, which were still quite weak.

3 May Anni-Frid and Benny made the most of a short stay in Stockholm to record two new tracks for the forthcoming *Frida Ensam* album. Five days later, Björn and Benny went back into the studio to finish a new version of 'Ring Ring', made especially for the English market. The original orchestration was enriched by a saxophone and extra guitars. In England, the *Waterloo* album was released on 17 May. It climbed no higher than No. 28.

'WE LISTEN TO OTHER PEOPLE'S MUSIC A LOT. THAT'S BY FAR THE GREATEST INSPIRATION WHILE WE'RE WRITING. WE WRITE VERY REGULARLY – MORE OR LESS OFFICE HOURS. AS FOR EQUIPMENT, WE'RE PRETTY FLEXIBLE. WE CAN WRITE WITH AN OLD GUITAR WITH OLD STRINGS, AND A BATTERED PIANO THAT'S OUT OF TUNE. BUT USUALLY WE TRY TO SET UP A FEW AMPS." **BJÖRN**

18 November Polar Music released the single 'So Long'. The Swedish public didn't take to this particular track immediately. The single did not enter the charts until 29 January 1975, eventually reaching No. 7. Benny says: 'It's not a good song at all. At this point, we wanted "Rock Me" as a single, but we were advised that with Björn singing, it would be difficult for people to identify it as an ABBA record.' (*The Complete Recording Sessions*, 1994.)

26 November Polydor released 'So Long' in Germany. The public's reaction was favourable: the record stayed in the charts for sixteen weeks and climbed to No. 11. From 'Ring Ring' onwards, ABBA would occupy a special place in the hearts of the German public. Radio Luxembourg named them Most Popular Group of the Year. During December, the four members of ABBA went to East Germany to record a TV show on which they would sing 'Waterloo', 'Honey Honey' and 'So Long'.

29 November 'So Long' was released in England, Belgium and France. ABBA travelled to Paris early the next year to promote the track. In Spain, the song reached No. 24. Unfortunately, ABBA were not able to make a promotional film for 'So Long' – the group were too busy touring at that time – as it would have been seen worldwide on television.

☆ ☆ ☆ ☆

The Polar Music empire was growing. Stig Anderson had just bought an exclusive hotel in the embassy district of Stockholm for a reputed 2.3 million Swedish kronor. The building, built in 1906, had belonged to Paul U. Bergström, the man behind the PUB department store. Stig wanted to turn this building into ABBA's headquarters. He had planned numerous alterations. The work would be supervised by his wife Gudrun. The total cost for the renovation and refitting was 1.5 million kronor.

☆ ☆ ☆ ☆

4 December ABBA were in London to record *Top of the Pops*. Despite a brilliant performance and several promotional pushes, 'So Long' didn't do very well in the British charts.

At the end of December, the group took a break on the island of Viggsö where Björn and Benny worked on new compositions such as 'I Do, I Do, I Do, I Do, I Do' and 'Tropical Loveland'.

The end-of-year accounts couldn't have been better. In France, the 'Waterloo' single was awarded a gold disc for sales exceeding 500,000 copies. In Belgium, it reached gold-disc status three months after its release. 'Waterloo' charted in fourteen countries, notably reaching No. 1 in the UK and No. 6 on the American *Billboard* chart – the United States having a reputation for being difficult to crack as far as pop music is concerned. Total global sales of the single were six million copies (of which 800,000 were in the United States). For its part, the album sold more than 3.5 million copies.

In the UK, the flop of 'Ring Ring' and the lukewarm reception given to 'Honey Honey' seemed to confirm the views of the British critics. From the start, they had said things like: 'ABBA won't survive Eurovision. They won the contest but they'll never be able to return to the top of the charts with another strong song. Nobody has ever made a career from it.' Stig took a different view: 'Even if we hadn't won, ABBA would still have had an international breakthrough. Things would have taken longer to have fallen into place, but we would still have made the charts. Don't forget that in the United States, Japan and Australia, nobody knows the Eurovision Song Contest!'

In Australia, the record company released two singles at the same time, 'So Long'/'Hasta Mañana' and 'I've Been Waiting For You'/'King Kong Song'. Stig commented: 'From "Ring Ring" onwards, the Australians appreciated ABBA. This year, "Waterloo" reached No. 4 and "Honey Honey" No. 30. The RCA representatives have told us that they'd like to meet the group.'

'EUROVISION REALLY JUST MADE THINGS HAPPEN FASTER FOR ABBA. IT WOULD HAVE HAPPENED REGARDLESS OF IT. AFTER ALL, AMERICA AND AUSTRALIA AREN'T INTERESTED IN THE EUROVISION.'
STIG

'FRIDA IS EXTREMELY TALENTED. SHE COULD HAVE BEEN A PROFESSIONAL DANCER WITHOUT ANY DOUBT. SHE MADE A LOT OF PROGRESS AND THIS GAVE HER AN EVEN BIGGER INTEREST. WHEN WE MEET WE DANCE AND DANCE, WE CAN'T STOP DANCING.' GRAHAM TAINTON ABBA'S CHOREOGRAPHER

The first part of the tour consisted of thirteen dates in several northern European countries. Surprisingly, no concerts were planned in Belgium or Holland, where ABBA had had considerable success.

NOVEMBER

Sunday	17	Copenhagen	**Falkonerteater**
Monday	18	Hanover	**Kuppelsaal**
Tuesday	19	Munich	**Deutsches Museum**

ABBA then played in Frankfurt, Berlin, Nuremberg (Germany), Innsbruck, Vienna (Austria), Zürich (Switzerland), Düsseldorf, Bremen and Hamburg (Germany). The last concert was on 30 November.

In Copenhagen, ABBA played to a full house, and the critics were favourable. The day after the premiere, Tore Ljunberg wrote in the daily newspaper *Arbetet*: 'Even if the sound level was too loud, the show was very well produced and the rhythm was brilliant.' Hans Fridlund said in *Expressen*: 'A dazzling show, both with colour and costumes, with very good choreography. The sound quality was perfect and the new songs are fantastic and very lively.' Thomas Walden remarked in *Aftonbladet*: 'The audience applauded politely, but there was no emotion, which is something I've often noticed in Denmark.'

The first two weeks of concerts had been disappointing. Apart from Copenhagen, ABBA played to half-empty houses. The Düsseldorf and Zurich concerts were cancelled because of low ticket sales. On top of this, Anni-Frid had a bad case of flu and feared that she would not be able to perform every night. However, thanks to their unfailing enthusiasm and energy, the four Swedes overcame these difficulties.

One German journalist wrote: 'Total entertainment. The shiny and glamorous ABBA performed a set that emphasized the visual. Björn sparkled in his overalls and his platform boots, higher than those of Dave Hill and Gary Glitter combined. The girls showed their bodies and sang in perfect two-part harmony. Vocally, ABBA have more resources than many other pop groups. Nevertheless, the audience's reception was lukewarm.' Gerald Büchelmaier wrote in *Bravo*: 'The high point of the show was the scant clothing. Until now, no group has bared so much of itself in Germany. The most courageous were Björn, in his glittery tights *à la* Mick Jagger and Anni-Frid in a skintight bolero and a mini-skirt slit into eighteen strips.'

The group kept something in reserve for the continuation of the tour. From a financial point of view, this first leg of the tour wasn't at all profitable. 'We thought that we would be turning some people away here and there,' explains Björn. 'Especially in Germany and in Austria, where our records were always at the top of the charts. We also thought that we would be singing in front of a younger audience. The majority of people in the crowd were at least twenty-five to thirty years old.'

After a long break and following a week's rehearsal at the Jarla theatre in Stockholm, ABBA went back on the road. From 10 to 22 January, they toured Scandinavia.

JANUARY

Friday	10	Oslo	**Chateau Neuf**
Saturday	11	Stockholm	**Konserthuset**
Sunday	12	Lund	**Olympen**
Friday	17	Copenhagen	**Tivoli Konsertsal**
Saturday	18	Gothenburg	**Scandinavium**
Monday	20	Helsinki	**Finlandia Hall**
Wednesday	22	Umeå	**Universum**

This second part of the tour was much more successful. The group played to packed houses every night. After the Oslo concert, Mats Olsson wrote in *Expressen*: 'ABBA has become a real stage group. In concert, "King Kong Song" is much more aggressive and has got more rhythm than on record. "Man In the Middle" is another song which works really well on stage, just as "I've Been Waiting For You", the highlight of ABBA's show, sung by Agnetha, sends shivers down your spine.' Critical opinion was divided, though, and the day after the show at the Konserthuset in Stockholm, Björn Levin wrote in daily newspaper GT: 'On stage, ABBA do no more than they do on record. The songs all follow each other, there are highs and lows – happy pop music, but nothing remarkable. The songs are nice to listen to, but after an hour it gets quite tedious.' *Aftonbladet* was more positive: 'Well that's it then – international group ABBA have achieved their breakthrough in Sweden. If you thought that the group's popularity was beginning to fade then you were wrong. They're more popular now than ever. When someone writes the history of seventies pop music, ABBA will come out on top.'

Björn has bad memories of the show they did in Stockholm: 'It's the worst onstage moment that I have ever experienced. It happened on "King Kong Song". When we came to one of the percussion breaks in the song, one of the girls started singing in the wrong place. One half of the band followed her,

'SOME OF THE TOURS WERE FULLY EQUIPPED WITH TWO OR THREE OR EVEN FOUR SAMPLES OF EACH COSTUME, SO THAT THEY COULD BE SHIFTED.' OWE SANDSTRÖM ABBA'S COSTUME DESIGNER

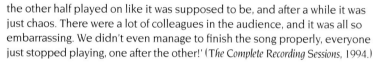
ABBA on stage in Germany

Liseberg, Gothenburg

the other half played on like it was supposed to be, and after a while it was just chaos. There were a lot of colleagues in the audience, and it was all so embarrassing. We didn't even manage to finish the song properly, everyone just stopped playing, one after the other!' (*The Complete Recording Sessions*, 1994.)

After the Stockholm concert, Agnetha, Björn, Benny and Anni-Frid met American producer Sid Bernstein (ex-producer of the Beatles in the USA). He couldn't stop showering them with praise: 'They're the Swedish Beatles. They've got a different style of song, they're young and are physically very attractive. That's very important in the United States!'

In Gothenburg, the Scandinavium theatre holds only 7,000 people; this greatly displeased director Bertil Rönnberg, who wanted to move the stage to allow a few thousand more people in. The day after the concert, Hans-Eric Åhman wrote in *Göteborgs-Posten*: 'A joy to both the eyes and the ears. This was a very classy show. There wasn't a single dull moment. The songs that hit you most are "I've Been Waiting For You", where the girls sing so high that it gives you goose pimples, and the gentle, melodic "Hasta Mañana". The group finish with "So Long" and "Waterloo" and it has the desired effect. The applause carried on for a long time after the show had ended. ABBA are the best we have in Sweden right now.'

In February 1975, following the success of the Scandinavian tour, Stig announced that ABBA would be extending it with a series of concerts in the Swedish parks during the summer.

Rehearsals began again on 1 June at the Jarla theatre. This time, guitarist Lasse Wellander joined the Beatmakers. During the show, which featured eighteen songs, Agnetha and Frida had several changes of costume, including some new creations by Owe and Lars: long dresses and short white tunics featuring blue and yellow cats.

JUNE

Saturday	21	Skellefteå	Folkets Park	20.00
Sunday	22	Sunderbyn	Sunderby Loge	19.30
Wednesday	25	Hudiksvall	Köpmanberget	21.00
Thursday	26	Björneborg, Finland	Folkets Park	22.00
Friday	27	Borlänge	Folkets Park	21.00
Saturday	28	Eskilstuna	Folkets Park	22.00
Monday	30	Stockholm	Gröna Lund	20.00

JULY

Tuesday	01	Linköping (cancelled and rescheduled for 8th July)		
Wednesday	02	Gamleby (cancelled and rescheduled for 9th July)		
Thursday	03	Malmö	Folkets Park	21.00
Friday	04	Storebro	Folkets Park	22.00
Saturday	05	Kristianopel	Masten	22.00
Sunday	06	Gothenburg	Liseberg	20.00
Monday	07	Borgholm	Slottsruinen	20.00
Tuesday	08	Linköping	Folkets Park	21.00
Wednesday	09	Gamleby	Folkets Park	21.30

Gröna Lund amusement park, Stockholm

Liseberg, Gothenburg

The two concerts in Linköping and Gamleby were postponed due to Agnetha having a bad case of tonsillitis – she was taken to Danderyd hospital with a temperature of 39.6°. Agnetha recalls: 'The evening in Malmö was a nightmare. My legs were shaking and 10 minutes before going on stage I broke down in tears in the dressing room. Luckily, I managed to keep going until the end of the show. Our doctor, Åke Olsson, was waiting backstage in case something happened to me.'

The day after the concert in Skellefteå, a disappointed Ricki Neuman wrote in *Aftonbladet*: 'We were waiting for something really exciting. There was lots of electricity but not much contact. No rapport between the artists and the audience. Even on stage there was no real communication. Except for Björn's comment about his wife: "She's got a really romantic voice and the sexiest bottom in Sweden!" '

Anders Björkman, in *Expressen*, had a quite different opinion: 'The whole show was a pleasure to watch. It was a real party, with fireworks, smoke and bubbles, all competing with the setting sun. The ABBA circus is without doubt a star attraction.' But Mia Gerdin wrote in *Dagens Nyheter*: 'I heard them sing, I saw them move, but they gave me the impression that they were lifeless. The ABBA show was a mixture of absurd contrasts.'

Despite these criticisms, the tour was a triumph. The audiences in the parks were full of admiration. Being used to more traditional shows, people were astonished when they witnessed the innovative special effects. The group attracted more than 100,000 spectators, with a record audience of 19,000 at the amusement park Gröna Lund in Stockholm.

1975

3 January ABBA made their long-awaited return to Swedish television, appearing on a TV show called *Nygammalt*, presented by Bosse Larsson. The group performed 'So Long' and 'I've Been Waiting For You'.

7–8 January Björn and Benny were in the studio putting the finishing touches to a new version of 'Bang-a-Boomerang' for Swedish duo Svenne and Lotta. The couple were to take part in the Swedish Eurovision heats the following February. Björn and Benny, not having had the time to compose an original song for the competition, had suggested arranging the song at a slightly faster tempo. Svenne and Lotta would record Swedish and English versions of 'Bang-a-Boomerang'.

10 January ABBA opened the second leg of their tour with a concert in Oslo. Stig confessed to *Kvällsposten*: 'We would have really liked it if Swedish Television had made the most of this tour and filmed the show. But we didn't get any positive response. Only one producer was interested in doing a programme with ABBA, but that project fell through due to financial problems.'

30 January The four Swedes went to Germany to sing 'So Long' on the very popular *Disco 75* TV show. Polydor presented the group with four gold discs, to acknowledge sales of two million copies of 'Waterloo'.

1 February ABBA arrived in Paris for three days of promotion. The group sang 'So Long' on the show *Samedi est à Vous* and then went on to RTL radio for the programme *Super Club*, where they performed 'Waterloo' and 'So Long'. During their stay in the French capital, Agnetha, Björn, Benny and Anni-Frid gave several interviews and attended various photo sessions. They were invited on to Guy Lux's *Système 2* programme. The clip of 'So Long' would be screened on 9 February.

At the beginning of February, Stig announced to the Swedish press that ABBA would follow their European tour with a series of fourteen concerts in the Swedish parks the following June and July. By doing this he put an end to the resentment felt by certain journalists who had accused the group of neglecting the Swedish public after the cancellation of the summer 1974 tour.

15 February Svenne and Lotta performed 'Bang-En-Boomerang' (Swedish version) in the 1975 Swedish Eurovision heats. They finished in third place, but this didn't prevent the record from becoming a big hit in Sweden. The B-side, 'Kom Ta En Sista Dans Med Mig' is the Swedish version of 'Dance (While the Music Still Goes On)', from ABBA's *Waterloo* album.

Agnetha, Bjorn, Benny and Anni-Frid devoted the months of February and March to the recording of the new album. For the sleeve, photographer Ola Lager shot the group in the Castle Hotel in Stockholm and in a limousine hired for the occasion. 'The idea came from Ron Spaulding, my artistic director at the time,' explains Ola Lager. 'The car is a 1952 Rolls-Royce which belonged to financial genius Torsten Kreuger. My wife took charge of the styling. Actually, you can see her in a black dress in the photos taken at the hotel. The other extras were Lars, the manager of the hotel, and his staff.'

At the end of March, the two couples allowed themselves some time off before setting out on a very heavy promotional schedule. Agnetha, Björn and Linda flew off for a week's holiday in Crete, in the village of Ayios Nikolaos. Anni-Frid and Benny chose Los Angeles in sunny California. While there, they had the chance to meet up with their friend Björn Skifs, who was touring the United States at that time with his group the Blue Swedes.

10 April 'I Do, I Do, I Do, I Do, I Do' was released. In London, Epic-CBS sent three promotions men to all the capital's radio stations. The men, dressed in dinner jackets, arrived by limousine and delivered the single to the DJs together with a bottle of champagne. Despite these efforts, the record didn't reach higher than No. 38 in the charts. It has to be said that the British press took great delight in knocking ABBA. The New Musical Express wrote: 'The melody is desperately ordinary.' Melody Maker didn't go overboard either: '"I Do, I Do, I Do …" is so bad it hurts.' The welcome was clearly better in other countries. The record reached No. 2 in Belgium, No. 6 in Germany and in Denmark, No. 5 in South Africa, No. 3 in Holland and No. 1 in Australia.

14 April ABBA performed 'I Do, I Do, I Do, I Do, I Do' and 'S.O.S.' on the Dutch TV show Top Pop. The former was then No. 3 in the Dutch Top 40.

15 April ABBA were in Brussels for the recording of the RTB show Chansons à la Carte. The group performed 'Rock Me' at the beginning of the show, and 'I Do, I Do, I Do, I Do, I Do' later on in the programme.

In France, 'I Do, I Do, I Do, I Do, I Do' received a lot of radio airplay. The four Swedes arrived in Paris from Brussels and appeared on the programmes Samedi est à Vous and Midi-Première. ABBA were to be seen again on 1 June, in a clip recorded for Guy Lux's Système 2 show.

'SOMETIMES, WHEN YOU HAVE A CATCHY HOOKLINE, YOU FIND THAT THE REPETITION OF WORDS IS VERY EFFECTIVE. WE USED TO FEEL THE TITLES MORE THAN, YOU KNOW, ACTUALLY MAKING IT IMPORTANT WHETHER THEY MEANT SOMETHING OR NOT!' BJÖRN

Chansons à la Carte, Brussels

'Rock Me', Chansons à la Carte, Brussels

After having recorded the promotional video for 'Mamma Mia' in the studio, ABBA filmed clips for three other songs: 'I Do, I Do, I Do, I Do, I Do', 'S.O.S.' and 'Bang-a-Boomerang'. The latter was recorded in the centre of Stockholm. 'We have to thank producer Lasse Hallström,' Björn emphasizes, 'because he was one of the pioneers in the field of videos. MTV and the other music channels didn't exist in those days. We had seen a really badly filmed promotional video from the United States where a single camera had filmed just one view. Lasse convinced us that we could do distinctly better. He already had lots of ideas in his head. Even if we sometimes added some ideas of our own, it was Lasse who found all the concepts and developed the synopsis. Today, these clips seem out of date. In 1975, we were among the first to record them.'

21 April The long-awaited new album, entitled Abba, was released simultaneously throughout Europe. For the first time, the melodies, voices, arrangements and sound recording combined to give the impression of exceptional harmony. You could say that this is where Björn, Benny and Michael B. Tretow revealed the 'new', almost-perfect ABBA sound, instantly recognizable as their own. One should also mention the innovative track 'Intermezzo No. 1', previously entitled 'Bach-låten' (Bach's Song), Benny's subtle tribute to his favourite classical composer. In Sweden, the album was a considerable success, going straight in at No. 1 on the Kvällstoppen chart on 29 April, staying in the charts for a total of forty-one weeks and selling 550,000 copies.

Mats Olsson wrote in Expressen: 'What is interesting is that ABBA have refined their style. The songs are stronger and give an impression of homogeneity. There are no longer any weak tracks. Björn and Benny have no equals in recording catchy, instantly memorable melodies. The lyrics don't carry any

'THE ABBA SOUND IS THE GIRLS – THEY ARE THE ONES YOU HEAR. BJÖRN AND I MAY CREATE THE WORDS, BUT THEY ARE THE ONES WHO MAKE THE SOUND. TAKE THEM AWAY AND YOU HAVE NO MORE ABBA. I THINK WE PIONEERED THAT SOUND.' BENNY

strong message but ABBA have never claimed that they do. Their music is superior to others. It's at the same time *schlager* and pop. Especially "I Do, I Do, I Do, I Do, I Do", which is without doubt their best song: marvellous saxophones, a melody, superb couplets and Agnetha's voice layered over Anni-Frid's in the chorus. And as far as the girls are concerned, yes, it's possible that Anni-Frid has the better voice, but Agnetha has a special stamp which I find tremendously seductive ("I've Been Waiting For You", for instance). I often play the album and you probably will do so too.'

In Britain, the press persisted with comments such as 'ABBA cannot survive the Eurovision Song Contest'. *Disc* magazine wrote: 'Poor ABBA seem to have had a lot of good intentions with this album. Certainly, it contains some songs which would make excellent singles, like "Bang-A-Boomerang", "I Do, I Do, I Do, I Do, I Do" and the excellent "So Long", but the rest do not deserve a mention.' However, despite the bad press, the record reached No. 13 on the British charts. Björn remembers: 'In 1975, the welcome in Britain had completely changed as opposed to the previous year. We really had to fight to command respect among Anglo-Saxon artists. When we appeared on the programme *Top of the Pops*, the British unions told us we weren't allowed to use our playback tapes which had been recorded using foreign musicians. It left us two solutions: record a new version using the show's musicians or perform completely live. One day we were in Manchester for ITV with the group Queen. Their performance, using their tape, was magnificent, but ours was very average. When "Waterloo" was No. I they put us in the best hotels and drove us around in a Rolls. Later on, the quality of the rooms we were given and the transport we used had really gone downhill.'

6 May ABBA were in the studio to record 'Medley'. Made up of three extracts of American folk songs, the track appeared on a German album entitled *Stars im Zeichen eines Guten Sterns*, for which all profits were donated to cancer research. 'We were asked if we would like to contribute a song to this album,' remembers Benny, 'and since it would take too much time to write a new song, we decided to record this medley of folk songs. It was fun to do it – we felt freer because it wasn't our own material, and I think it turned out quite well.' (*The Complete Recording Sessions*, 1994.)

22–23 May Agnetha, Björn, Benny and Anni-Frid were in Hamburg to take part in the TV show *Disco 75*. After the recording, they were presented with gold discs acknowledging sales of 'Honey Honey' in Germany.

25 May ABBA were in Paris to sing 'I Do, I Do, I Do, I Do, I Do' on the programme *Système* 2. The clip was recorded in advance and screened on 1 June. On the RTL charts, they climbed no higher than No. 26. However, the single was awarded a gold disc. (A little clarification is necessary as far as the French charts are concerned. Unlike a lot of countries, French chart placings were not based on record sales up until 1984. They were produced by the directors of programme planning for private radio stations and inevitably were not representative of sales or the tastes of the general public. They were also based on other factors: the tastes of the programme planners, affinities with record companies, publishing contracts, and so on. In ABBA's case, the group sold lots of records, were often played on the radio and on TV, but their chart positions didn't reflect this.)

27 May The group were in Copenhagen to take part in the programme *Omkring Et Flygel*, on which they sang 'S.O.S.' and 'So Long', and hummed 'Alleycat'. During the afternoon there was a presentation of gold discs and a photo session at the famous Tivoli Gardens.

3 June The single 'S.O.S.' was released simultaneously in Sweden and the United States. In Belgium, it was released at the end of the month and reached No. I on 5 July. There were excellent results, too, across the Rhine: the song, having reached No. I, stayed in the German charts for more than seven months.

During the month of June, the Polish President, Edward Gierek, was in Sweden for a visit which lasted several days. In Poland, the press widely covered this visit and dedicated numerous articles to the host country. This led to one daily newspaper publishing a photo of ABBA along with the address of the Swedish fan club. In a few weeks, dozens of sackloads of post would arrive at the group's Stockholm headquarters containing letters, poems, pictures and hand-made objects paying homage to ABBA. Amusingly, the Polish fans, taking Björn to be a woman, portrayed him with breasts. In response to this tidal wave of interest, Stig took steps to distribute the group's records in Poland and East Germany. His concern was not only that the record companies in these countries were controlled by the state, but that the annual budget was allotted to limited imports. As Stig explained: 'We pressed 250,000 copies of the *Abba* album especially for Poland, while the demand was four times greater. As a result, these financial restrictions increased sales of ABBA's records on the black market.'

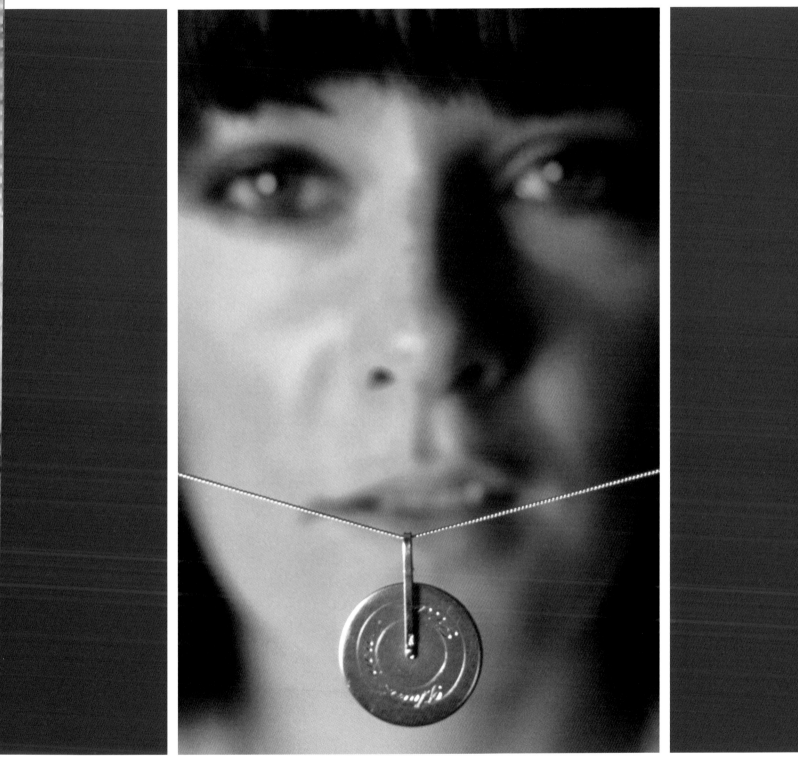

'WHEN I WAS THIRTY, I FELT VERY TRAPPED: I THINK IT'S SOMETHING MOST WOMEN GO THROUGH. I READ SOMEWHERE THAT AT TWENTY YOU MAKE UP YOUR MIND WHAT YOU WANT FROM LIFE AND AT THIRTY YOU CHANGE AND QUESTION EVERYTHING. EVERYTHING WAS UPSIDE-DOWN FOR ME. I HAD NO CONFIDENCE IN MYSELF. AT THE SAME TIME, YOU MUST GO ON WORKING. IT LASTED ABOUT A YEAR.' FRIDA

'"MAMMA MIA" IS VERY IMPORTANT TO ME BECAUSE THAT VIDEO REALLY BROKE IT IN AUSTRALIA AND AFTER THAT, IN '76, THINGS REALLY WENT ABSOLUTELY WILD AT ONE POINT. EVERY TENTH OF THE POPULATION, EVERY TENTH INHABITANT WOULD BUY AN ABBA RECORD, WHICH IS AN INCREDIBLE RECORD. I DON'T THINK THAT HAS HAPPENED ANYWHERE ELSE WITH ANYONE ELSE.' **BJÖRN**

1 December   CBS-Cupol released Agnetha's *Elva Kvinnor I Ett Hus* (Eleven Women In a House) album. It was the singer's last record on this label. Apart from 'S.O.S.', all the lyrics were written by Bosse Carlgren and the music composed by Agnetha. She also produced the entire album. Mats Olsson wrote in *Expressen*: 'I like Agnetha Fältskog. She has a voice which has gone straight to my heart since her first hit in 1967. I'd like to be able to say that it's a great album, but I can't. I like Agnetha when she sings sad ballads and songs of genuine sorrow. Here, she has to fight to be able to be heard (and she doesn't manage it!). Is it because the album wants to be taken seriously? Musically, it's quite an original record (good melodies, good arrangements and a different production to ABBA) which deserves genuine lyrics and not clichés pulled out of a hat. Fortunately, the second side makes up for the rest with tracks like "Mina Ögon", "Dom Har Glömt" and "Visa I Åttonde Månaden". I'd prefer to learn more about Agnetha rather than a crowd of fake people in a house which doesn't even exist!'

In view of the way that ABBA's career was taking off, Stig insisted that Agnetha and Frida did no TV promotion for their respective albums. He was relieved to see the end of the contract which tied Agnetha to her record company. From now on, he would be able to remove the credit 'Agnetha by courtesy of CBS-Cupol AB' from all the group's records.

4–5 December   The group were in Germany for the recording of a New Year's Eve show. There was a real party atmosphere as ABBA sang 'I Do, I Do, I Do, I Do, I Do', 'S.O.S.', 'Mamma Mia' and 'Waterloo' in front of an audience.

During December, Björn and Benny completed the recording of Ted Gardestad's new album *Franska Kort* (French Card), which they had begun in August. The record was co-produced by Michael B. Tretow. Frida contributed backing vocals on some songs.

8 December   Agnetha had an operation on her tonsils. After having to put the date back several times due to time constraints, she finally chose this time of year which was more favourable for resting. 'I couldn't wait any longer,' remembers Agnetha. 'Since childhood, I had suffered from repetitive tonsillitis and throat problems. Because of that, I almost jeopardized our participation in the Eurovision Song Contest in Brighton. On tour, I was always afraid of an infection. It became an obstacle to our career. Of course, the operation was painful, in view of my age. For the following two or three weeks I didn't say a single word. I was so afraid that my voice would change!'

10 December   The single 'I Do, I Do, I Do, I Do, I Do' was released in the United States. Its climb up the American charts was slow but sure: the song remained in the charts for eight weeks and reached No. 15 in May 1976.

The year finished brilliantly for ABBA. All the effort put into promotion paid off. In most countries, the group improved on their success or managed to pick up again where their popularity had been foundering.

In the United States, 'S.O.S.' sold more than a million copies. As a result of numerous TV appearances the group became better known and appreciated by American audiences. They also did a lot of TV and radio promotion in France, where, even if their songs did not always reach the top of the charts, as they did in Belgium, their records sold relatively well. After 'I Do, I Do, I Do, I Do, I Do' (silver disc), 'S.O.S.' received a gold disc, and the youth press (*Salut Les Copains*, *Stéphanie*, *Hit Magazine*) were becoming more and more interested in ABBA. It was a successful year in Belgium: 'I Do, I Do, I Do, I Do, I Do' reached No. 2, 'S.O.S.' No. 1, and 'Mamma Mia' had been at No. 2 since 12 December. They spent a total of thirty-one weeks in the Belgian charts. In Germany, 'S.O.S.' was voted Best Song of the Year. And in Britain, 'S.O.S.' and especially 'Mamma Mia' had put a smile back on the faces of British fans.

We added "S.O.S." [performed "live" in 1975] because of time constraints. The programme was broadcast in more than thirty countries.'

2–3 February The group were in the studio with director Lasse Hallström to record the promotional film for 'Fernando'. ABBA went for the simple approach, with lots of long shots of them sitting around a fire. This new track gave the fans the chance to see Benny playing the guitar. They made a small mistake with their English on 'Fernando', singing 'since many years …' instead of 'for many years …', which amused the British audience. At the same time, Lasse Hallström recorded the video for 'Dancing Queen', which was filmed at the Alexandra discotheque.

Musikladen TV special, Germany

22 February The French audience had their first chance to hear the new ABBA song 'Fernando'. ABBA were invited to appear on Guy Lux's *Système* 2 show, live from the Sporting-Club in Monte Carlo. Two days later, Agnetha, Björn, Benny and Anni-Frid were in Paris to appear on *Midi-Première*. 'Fernando' entered the RTL charts on 20 March and stayed there for three months, peaking at No. 3. The single was awarded a gold disc. It was ABBA's best performance in France since 'Waterloo'.

28 February The group were in Germany to record the programme *Disco 76*. During this time, Polydor released the single 'Fernando'. The track would stay in the charts for seven months. It reached No. 1 on 29 March. The German public had taken ABBA to their hearts. Since their victory in Brighton, the group's fans had seen several compilations released by Polydor: *Honey Honey*, *Best of Abba*, *The Very Best of Abba*, *Mamma Mia* and *Pop Power*.

Gold disc for ABBA in Australia

4–14 March Agnetha, Björn, Benny and Anni-Frid paid their first visit to Australia. The welcome they received as they stepped off the plane took them by surprise. The girls were moved to tears. The airport was besieged by about a thousand fans, all shouting and chanting for the group. Even the police, complete with reinforcements, had trouble controlling the crowd. The following day, the newspaper headlines read 'ABBA Fever Hits Australia'. The television news even devoted 8 minutes to a report on what they called 'The most important musical event since the Beatles'. In his report, the journalist said: 'This continent hasn't been touched by a phenomenon like this since Hurricane Tracey.' The group had brought along Thomas Johansson (EMA-Telstar) on this promotional trip; he was in charge of organizing the future tour of Europe and Australia. Journalist Hans Fridlund was also with them. Each day he sent an update on 'ABBA in Australia' by telex to *Expressen* for the next day's paper.

After Melbourne, the group travelled to Sydney. In ten days, they took part in press conferences, autograph-signing sessions, radio interviews and TV shows (notably A *Current Affair*, *Bandstand* and *Celebrity Squares*). The Australians had been waiting so long for this visit and the welcome that ABBA received was so warm that the group found it hard to refuse the numerous requests which came in. There is a story that before ABBA's arrival, many Australians believed that Agnetha and Frida were two models who were there to enhance the group's image and that Björn and Benny had used two very accomplished but less attractive singers in the studio!

Frida at a press conference, Australia

One of the high points of this trip was the recording of a TV show. Two months earlier, several companies had been fighting over exclusive rights. It was eventually Network 9 who won the rights to record the programme. Stig had negotiated airline tickets and first-class accommodation in luxurious hotels for the whole entourage. The television company pulled off a real coup: when the programme was first shown, it was watched by 58 per cent of the viewing public, more than had watched the first moon landing in 1969!

In the televised show, the group performed their biggest hits, with several costume changes. There are actually two versions of the show. In the first, intended for selling abroad and entitled *Abba In Australia*, outside shots

'THE BASIC THING IS TO BE VERY HONEST, NOT TO SELL AS MANY RECORDS AS POSSIBLE. THE MAIN THING IS TO DO WHAT YOU THINK IS THE BEST YOU CAN DO ALL THE TIME.'
BENNY

'Tropical Loveland', Musikladen TV special, Germany

'THE CLOTHES ARE DESIGNED BY OWE SANDSTRÖM AND LARS WIGENIUS. WE MEET REGULARLY. WE TALK AND SKETCH, I OFTEN COME UP WITH IDEAS. WE TRY TO REACH AN AGREEMENT AMONG OURSELVES ABOUT SOMETHING ALL OF US THINK IS GOOD. WE TOTALLY TRUST OWE AND LARS IN QUESTIONS OF QUALITY AND MATERIALS.' **FRIDA**

were mixed in with studio recordings of the songs. Agnetha, Björn, Benny and Anni-Frid were shown at Sydney zoo, on a boat on the Hawkesbury River, having a barbecue at the water's edge and trying to throw a boomerang during the song 'Tropical Loveland'. The second version, for Australian audiences, was filmed entirely in the studio and entitled The Best of ABBA. The show was screened numerous times in Australia and was bought by several television companies around the world.

At the end of ABBA's visit, Vicki Jones, publicity manager for Sydney's TCN-9, declared: 'I have never worked with such an agreeable group of people. Their schedule made them go at a killing pace – but they never once complained. And they were always on time for every appointment. The sort of image they present on screen – friendly, warm, bright, intelligent people – is exactly what they are.' Tony Culliton, the producer/director of the TV special, added: 'They were incredibly easy to get along with. They took direction well, but being professionals, had some suggestions of their own which always worked well. Complete modesty is the group's most refreshing quality.'

13 March 'Fernando' reached No. 1 in Belgium. The record stayed in the charts for four months. A survey revealed that ABBA were the most popular group in Belgium.

23–24 March ABBA recorded two new tracks at the Metronome studios: 'Knowing Me, Knowing You' and 'That's Me'. Of 'Knowing Me, Knowing You', Benny says: 'I think this ranks as one of our five best recordings.' And 'That's Me' is still one of Agnetha's favourite songs. (The Complete Recording Sessions, 1994.)

26 March The compilation album Greatest Hits was released in Britain. It was one of the first records to benefit from a television advertising campaign. There were four unreleased songs on this album: 'He Is Your Brother', 'People Need Love', 'Another Town, Another Train' and 'Nina, Pretty Ballerina'. The album had already sold so many copies through advance orders that it went straight into the charts. Greatest Hits stayed at No. 1 for nine weeks.

3 April The album Frida Ensam reached No. 1 in Sweden. It remained on the Svensktoppen chart for forty weeks.

5 April ABBA attended Expressen's Spring Party, at the Operakällaren restaurant in Stockholm. The group celebrated Agnetha's twenty-sixth birthday at this event, together with Stig and numerous other guests.

During April, ABBA made a brief promotional visit to France. The group performed 'Fernando' on the programmes Ring Parade and Midi-Première. Vogue released a new pressing of the Greatest Hits compilation, with 'Fernando' as a bonus track. After several months, the record was awarded a gold disc.

Expressen published some astounding figures at this time: 'Since the group's visit to Australia, "ABBAmania" has grown even further. The four Swedes have now managed the achievement of having five singles and two albums in the charts at the same time. "Fernando" is at No. 1 and "Ring Ring" is a new entry on the chart at No. 4. "Rock Me" is at No. 5, "Mamma Mia" is at No. 20 and "S.O.S." is at No. 22.' 'Fernando' would actually stay at No. 1 for fifteen weeks. The record for the most weeks at No. 1 in Australia was held by the Beatles with 'Hey Jude', which was at the top for sixteen weeks. In the album charts, Abba was at No. 1 and The Best of Abba at No. 2. The TV programme The Best of Abba was screened several times in Australia. Public demand was so great, however, that the television stations went so far as to buy footage from German and French television. An Australian TV crew was even sent to Stockholm to make a programme called Abba In Sweden.

In the United States, ABBA's records were often released in a different order to the rest of the world. While 'Fernando' was having great success all over Europe, 'I Do, I Do, I Do, I Do, I Do' was at No. 15 in America. On 3 May,

'Fernando', ABBA In Australia TV special

Blaupunkt advertising campaign, Sweden

Atlantic released 'Mamma Mia' as a single. It got as high as No. 32 in the charts. Album sales were not as encouraging, since the Abba album hadn't even made the Top 150.

3 May The TV show *Made In Sweden For Export* (featuring ABBA, Björn Skifs, Sylvia Vrethammar and Lill Lindfors) was shown at the Golden Rose Of Montreux festival. The BBC won first prize.

8 May 'Fernando' managed to knock 'Save Your Kisses For Me', by the 1976 Eurovision winners Brotherhood of Man, off the No.1 spot in the British charts.

ABBA's Eurovision win inspired many imitators. First there was the Brotherhood of Man – two boys and two girls who tried to be 'the new ABBA' but, despite their Eurovision success, didn't manage to keep up the momentum. Then there were the two couples who made up Bucks Fizz, winners of the 1981 Eurovision Song Contest. In Holland, there was Teach-In, Luv' and, especially, the group Champagne, with their songs 'Valentino' and 'Oh Me, Oh My, Goodbye'. These groups tried to copy the ABBA image and sound, but the magic was always missing.

19 May An awful rumour that ABBA had been involved in a plane crash at Berlin's Tempelhof airport caused panic among German fans. Two days later, Polydor Germany's representative told newspaper *Expressen*: 'After having called Polar Music, I have spent the whole day trying to deny this stupid rumour, but it has already reached neighbouring countries. The bigger it gets, the more distorted it becomes. In Denmark and Holland, they're talking about three members of the group being killed in a plane crash. They're adding that Frida was the sole survivor but that she's now unable to sing any more because she is so badly injured.' Björn said of the situation: 'I can't explain these rumours. Agnetha and myself have often stated that we travel separately by plane because of the children. Maybe someone wanted to make fun of us?'

18 June ABBA paid tribute to a very special couple. King Carl XVI Gustav of Sweden would be marrying Silvia Sommerlath the following day. A huge gala had been organized at the Stockholm Opera House. The event was televised live and featured a host of prestigious Swedish stars like Birgit Nilsson, Kjerstin Dellert, Sven-Bertil Taube, Alice Babs and Elisabeth Söderström. ABBA were also among the artists performing. The group chose to perform the obvious song: 'Dancing Queen'. In honour of the occasion, Agnetha, Björn, Benny and Anni-Frid swapped their stage gear for costumes from the eighteenth century. Their performance captured the imagination of the audience and television viewers alike, but the press laid into ABBA in their

reports. Björn explains: 'They complained about us on the one hand for having written "Dancing Queen" for the future Queen Silvia, which wasn't the case because we had started recording this song a year earlier. On the other hand, the journalists used the gala to throw open the question of us performing live again. They were annoyed with us because we were the only ones to use playback during the show, whilst the other artists sang with the Royal Orchestra. We would have loved to have used the court musicians, but how could they really have reproduced the sound of our song?' At the end of the gala, the King, his fiancée and their entourage went on to Drottningholm Palace, where a grand banquet was held. The 300 guests, including the four members of ABBA, were invited to a huge dinner-dance at the Operakällaren restaurant.

July Björn, Benny and Thomas Johansson of EMA-Telstar travelled to London to make plans for a concert in 1977. Björn had the massive Earl's Court Arena in mind, having attended a Rolling Stones concert there, but they eventually settled on the Royal Albert Hall.

During the summer, the Australian television station Network 7 sent a camera crew to Sweden. Having failed to secure exclusive rights to *Abba In Australia*, the company had decided to make an hour-long programme entitled *Abba In Sweden*. Journalist Ian Meldrum interviewed the four members of ABBA on a boat moored in Stockholm port. Numerous clips were filmed around the capital, as well as an interview with Stig and radio presenter Ulf Elfving. For the songs, the company purchased footage from the TV show *Musikladen – The Best of Abba*. The show *Abba In Sweden* was screened in Australia on 30 September.

August ABBA recorded five adverts for the Japanese company National. The recording took place in Stockholm, in the ballroom of the Grand Hotel, with the outside shots being filmed near Drottningholm Palace. The song 'Fernando' had been reworked with new lyrics to promote the brand name National. Each little advert featured one of a range of products, from a hi-fi to various other household appliances. The Japanese company invested a million Australian dollars in the twelve-month campaign for Australian television, mainly in Melbourne and Sydney. 'Lots of companies wanted to use our name or a photo of ABBA in their advertising,' explained Stig. 'I was always against it. We made an exception with the company National because it gave us the opportunity to finance part of the Australian tour, and the products didn't do any harm to the group's image. It's more acceptable to see ABBA singing the praises of hi-fi equipment than tights or sweets!' Despite this declaration from Stig, the group were still seen publicizing Lois jeans and Blaupunkt and taking part in the Australian environmental campaign Keep Australia Beautiful.

6 August 'Dancing Queen' was released in Britain. It was an instant hit. It reached No. 1 on 4 September and stayed there for six consecutive weeks. The record sales figures were massive. Stig told the following story: 'One day, I found a note in my office with a telephone number. I gave the piece of paper to Görel and told her, "I don't know who it is, but can you call them anyway." Görel replied: "It's not a telephone number, it's the latest sales figures for 'Dancing Queen' in Britain!"'

13 August Vogue released the 'Dancing Queen' single in France and Belgium. The song reached No. 1 in Belgium on 21 August and would stay in the charts for fourteen weeks. This record introduced the whole world to the group's new logo. 'This was the second time that I'd worked with ABBA,' remembers Rune Söderqvist. 'Together with photographer Ola Lager, we thought that they needed an identifiable logo, since the record companies around the world were just doing anything with the design. For a long time I'd been talking to them about a real ABBA logo, easily identifiable and easy to use on any publicity material. I showed them about ten different slides with the reversed "B", each one totally different. I remember that Benny thought that the logo was "too industrial". I told him that this was my job and that he could trust me. I was subsequently proved right. The new logo was adopted from the "Dancing Queen" single onwards. Stig, who understood how powerful it could be, asked me to put it at the top of the record sleeve. This would mean that ABBA's albums could be instantly found on the shelves of the record stores.'

For the first time, Swedish Television was to dedicate a whole programme to ABBA. The documentary, entitled *Abba-Dabba-Dooo!!*, coincided with the launch of the new *Arrival* album and showed a different side of the group. In the middle of August, the four Swedes were filmed and interviewed by Per Falkman on the island of Viggsö. During the same month, several recording sessions took place at the Metronome studios, and Björn and Benny had the chance to complete tracks like 'My Love, My Life', 'Why Did It Have To Be Me' and the instrumental piece 'Arrival'.

16 August Polar Music released the 'Dancing Queen' single. Eight days later, the song was No. 1, staying at the top of the charts for fourteen weeks. More than 150,000 copies were sold in Sweden. 'In the beginning, we had decided not to release the track before the *Arrival* album,' explained Stig. 'But we changed our minds following the hundreds of requests which came in from everywhere. Everyone wanted to buy "the wedding song"!'

18 August Mats Olsson wrote in *Expressen*: 'Is "Dancing Queen" going to be a new worldwide hit, after the enormous success of "Fernando"? I don't know! But the song doesn't have the immediate effect of "Ring Ring", "Waterloo" or

"Mamma Mia" on the listener. On the other hand, though, it's certainly ABBA's best production so far. The attention to tiny detail and the girls' way of singing are becoming ABBA's trademark.' Anni-Frid remembers: 'I loved the song from the very beginning. Coming back from the studio, Benny played the backing track for me. It was so beautiful that I started to cry. I mean, even without lyrics or voices on it, it was outstanding.' As for the song's rhythm, Björn and Benny never concealed the fact that they were influenced by George McCrae's hit 'Rock Your Baby'.

21 August *Musikladen – The Best of Abba* was screened nationwide in Germany. Polydor made the most of the occasion by releasing the double compilation album *The Very Best of Abba*. The sleeve featured a series of stills from the TV show. In the programme, the group were interviewed and performed their biggest hits, changing costumes for each song.

26 August Vogue released the *Golden Double Album*. The French and Belgian fans had their first chance to hear 'Love Isn't Easy (But It Sure Is Hard Enough)', one of the group's early songs.

During September, the group continued filming for *Abba-Dabba-Dooo!!*. The crew made short film clips for some of the songs and interviewed each member of the group. The sections of ABBA singing live with an orchestra were recorded in a studio at the end of September.

1 September Agnetha, Björn, Benny and Anni-Frid attended the premiere of Lasse Berghagen's show at the Cabaret Berns in Stockholm.

2 September The centre of Stockholm witnessed a demonstration which said a great deal about ABBA's popularity in Sweden. At the beginning of the afternoon, a group of young people, with placards and a portable cassette player, marched around the streets of the capital announcing that the group ABBA would be visiting the steps of the Konserthuset at 4 o'clock that afternoon. The area around the theatre was soon invaded by several hundred people chanting: 'ABBA, we want to see ABBA!' The police, realizing the extent of the problem, finally put up barriers to contain the crowd. But the ABBA fans were disappointed when it all turned out to be a joke.

☆ ☆ ☆ ☆

with thirty-two gold, platinum and silver discs for the group's sales in Britain, plus a diamond disc for the 1,250,000 copies sold of *Greatest Hits*. The festivities were brought to a close by Epic-CBS announcing to the group that, only four days after the single's release, 'Money, Money, Money' had already sold 300,000 copies.

In Australia, ABBA pulled off an unprecedented achievement by having three albums simultaneously in the Top 30. The compilation *The Best of Abba* had already sold 860,000 copies, and even before its release the *Arrival* album (which in Australia featured 'Fernando') had sold 750,000 copies through advance orders. Australian TV had screened *Abba-Dabba-Dooo!!* on 26 October, long before other channels around the world would do so.

The *Melbourne Star* wrote: 'There is no doubt that *Arrival* is ABBA's best album and that they're going to earn lots of "Money, Money, Money".' The *Sydney Gazette* said: 'They definitely have a style which is instantly recognizable. This could be the reason why they are the kings and queens of current pop.'

Even Stig Anderson, who never concealed his taste for making money, couldn't believe it. 'I was astounded,' he said. 'A few years ago, I promised Björn and Benny that with my help they would one day be famous outside Scandinavia. But I could never have imagined such success. We are now selling well everywhere, except for China, North Korea and Vietnam.' On the other hand, ABBA fell victim to intense piracy. A stock of 700,000 pirated albums were discovered in Australia. The records, of an inferior quality, had the same sleeves as the originals but in black and white.

20 November ABBA were back at the top of the Belgian charts. 'Money, Money, Money' was the fifth single by the group to reach No. 1 in Belgium.

23 November ABBA made a brief visit to Holland. The four Swedes were invited to take part in the TV show *Een Van De Acht*, presented by Mies Bouwman, on which they performed 'Money, Money, Money', 'When I Kissed the Teacher' and 'Why Did It Have To Be Me', wearing their famous kimonos. Before the recording of the programme, the group were presented with numerous gold and platinum discs at a press conference.

24 November ABBA were in Paris to record two songs for *Les Rendez-Vous du Dimanche*. The first of these, 'Money, Money, Money' was screened on 28 November, while the second, 'When I Kissed the Teacher', would be screened on 2 January. 'Money, Money, Money' had just entered the RTL charts. It stayed there for twelve weeks, reaching No. 1 on 22 January 1977.

Rehearsals for the 1977 tour began at Grünewaldsalen, a room at the Konserthuset in Stockholm. Curiously, the tour wouldn't include Stockholm, although there were two concerts at the Scandinavium in Gothenburg. The 20,000 tickets sold out several hours after they went on sale. Stig told the press at this time: 'I have said to everyone that ABBA are not available for anything between April and October next year. Björn and Benny must have peace and quiet to write new songs for the new album.'

27–31 December Swedish radio station P3 broadcast a series of five programmes recorded that September: A för Agnetha Fältskog, B för Benny Andersson, B för Björn Ulvaeus, A för Anni-Frid Lyngstad and The Abba Story. On New Year's Eve, Agnetha, Björn and some of their friends were out drinking champagne at the Alexandra club, before it closed for the last time. Their friend Alexandra Charles, the owner of the club, would later open another establishment bearing the same name.

If 1975 had been a turning point for ABBA, 1976 was without doubt a year of great success, and one of the most important of their career. With such strong songs as 'Mamma Mia', 'Fernando' and 'Dancing Queen', the group had carved out a place for themselves among the world's biggest music stars and discredited the people who had claimed that ABBA were just a one-hit wonder.

In the United States, sales of the *Greatest Hits* album exceeded 500,000 copies. *Cashbox* magazine had just awarded them the prize Top LP and Singles Artists of the Year. ABBA had also received awards galore in Britain. The figures spoke for themselves: 1,250,000 copies sold of *Greatest Hits*. The *Arrival* album, released at the beginning of November, had already sold 450,000 copies and sales of 'Dancing Queen' were approaching 850,000. *The Sun*, having already named them Top TV Entertainers of the Year, awarded them the prize of Top Artists of the Year. Three ABBA tracks were in the paper's Top 10 chart, voted by the readers. Another tribute came from broadsheet *The Times*, which published a long article analysing ABBA's career.

In Britain, ABBA's huge popularity was clearly demonstrated by what had happened in November, when it was announced that two concerts would take place on 14 February 1977 at the Royal Albert Hall. Tickets had gone on sale by mail application only. For the 11,212 available seats, the organizers received an astonishing 3,500,000 ticket applications! It was therefore no exaggeration when David Hamilton introduced ABBA on *Top of the Pops* in December as 'the hottest group in the world'. Showbusiness professionals in Britain often used Stig as an example of successful management. Garth Pearce wrote in the *Daily Express*: 'Stig has built up a relatively small organization that ABBA themselves control 100 per cent. ABBA is actually a model, and there are many within the British music industry who have begun to reassess their views after seeing how ABBA is run. What England needs is one or two Stig Andersons.'

In Sweden, sales were also surprising for a country with a population of only nine million people. The *Arrival* album (which had been at the top of the chart for the last ten weeks) had already sold 770,000 copies. The *Greatest Hits* compilation had sold around 300,000. *Expressen*'s annual survey revealed that its readers considered *Abba-Dabba-Dooo!!* to be the Best Television Programme of 1976; the prize would be presented to the group the following spring. Last but not least, a journalist declared that ABBA were the second-biggest Swedish export after Volvo.

In other countries, sales of the *Arrival* album were also exceptional: 800,000 copies in Australia, 225,000 in Denmark, 130,000 in Norway and 52,000 in Finland. In Holland, the cassette *The Best of Abba* was the biggest seller of all time. In Belgium, *Arrival* was awarded a gold disc. In France, the compilation *Golden Double Album* received a gold disc and *Arrival* would receive a platinum disc a few months later. In Turkey, the public voted ABBA Group of the Year.

Mick Farren of the *New Musical Express* summed up the general attitude of the British press towards the four Swedes thus: 'I'd dismissed ABBA until a couple of my noble colleagues pointed out just how complex the ABBA backing tracks were. They were right. It took quite a while to strip away the eager, healthy vocal sound. Once that's done, you're actually left with pop structure in the grand manner of the Beatles or Phil Spector.'

'"MONEY, MONEY, MONEY" WAS A MASTERPIECE AS GOOD AS BEETHOVEN AND BACH. IT IS BANAL SONGS SUCH AS THEIRS WHICH HELP FURTHER MANKIND'S UNDERSTANDING OF MANKIND. THE SONGS WERE BRILLIANTLY CONSTRUCTED. ABBA IS ART.' **PHILIP HAUENSTEIN** MUSIC LECTURER

'THEY ARE A LIVING LEGEND. IN BRITAIN, IT'S ROUGHLY RECKONED THAT ONE IN EVERY TEN HOMES HAS AN ABBA RECORD IN THE FAMILY VINYL COLLECTION.' HARRY DOHERTY *NEW MUSICAL EXPRESS*

1977

At the beginning of the year, ABBA were awarded numerous prizes for their chart successes during 1976. In Britain, the *New Musical Express* announced that ABBA were now selling more records than either Paul McCartney or Rod Stewart. While *Arrival* was named Best Album of the Year by *Hitmakers* magazine, the readers of *Record Mirror* voted ABBA as their Top Group. The *Daily Express* wrote: 'ABBA are the biggest pop act since the Beatles.' In Holland, 'Dancing Queen' was named the Top Single of 1976. In Portugal, the same trophy went to 'Fernando', and Benny and Björn were awarded the prize for Top Producers and Top Songwriters.

Agnetha and Björn had been talking privately for some time about the possibility of having a second child. So as not to interfere too much with ABBA's career, they decided that it would be best if they planned the birth. After having consulted Stig, as well as the other people around them, they agreed that the most appropriate time would be at the end of the year. The couple, who had been living in Vallentuna for several years, had recently moved to the island of Lidingö, north-east of Stockholm.

4 January The *Arrival* album was released in the United States. It reached No. 20 and would remain in the charts for a total of fifty weeks. *Arrival* was the first ABBA album to be awarded a gold disc on the other side of the Atlantic.

12 January Björn, Benny, Stig and Thomas Johansson travelled to London to finalize details for the British concerts and especially for the shows at the Royal Albert Hall.

In response to journalists who constantly talked about 'ABBA's fortune', Stig announced: 'We are always investing money. For instance, we have just bought an art company, AH-Grafik, and also an art gallery. We're also planning on building a recording studio. Because of costs and timing, it would be much easier if we could work in our own studio. As far as the tour is concerned, it's going to cost between 1.3 and 1.5 million Swedish kronor. We won't make any profit from it at all, but it's important that the fans see ABBA on stage. It's also excellent promotion for the group and will generate record sales.'

In Stockholm, Agnetha and Anni-Frid were supervising the preparation of stage costumes with Owe Sandström and Lars Wigenius. Rehearsals had just resumed at the Europa Films studios in Bromma, near Stockholm. There was just a two-day break to record the promotional film for the next single, 'Knowing Me, Knowing You'. Lasse Hallström recorded the video in the snow, on the island of Lidingö. The indoor shots were filmed in a studio. Once again, the director's trademark style was evident, with long fixed shots highlighting the faces and profiles of the group. ABBA come across as being more sensual than in previous videos.

22 January 'Money, Money, Money' reached No. 1 on the French RTL chart; this was the first time that ABBA had reached the top of the radio station's chart. The song would go on to receive a gold disc. The group had appeared on Michel Drucker's *Les Rendez-Vous du Dimanche* show on 2 January. The clip, showing ABBA dressed in their kimono outfits performing 'When I Kissed the Teacher', had been recorded during the group's flying visit to Paris the previous November.

After rehearsing for several weeks during December and January, ABBA started their European tour, leaving Stockholm for Oslo on the evening of 26 January. The first concert took place at the Ekebergshallen two days later. The climax of the European tour would be the Royal Albert Hall shows on 14 February. (See '1977 Tour' chapter.)

'IT WAS SAID
THAT WE WERE
ALWAYS FALLING
OUT AND IT
WAS ABSOLUTELY
NOT TRUE.
I CANNOT EVEN
REMEMBER AN
AGGRESSIVE
MOMENT
BETWEEN US.'
FRIDA

'ARTICLES HAVE
SPECULATED
THAT FRIDA
AND I HATED
EACH OTHER
FROM THE START,
WHICH IS,
IN FACT, PURE
NONSENSE.
DURING OUR
ABBA CAREER,
WE ALWAYS
SUPPORTED
EACH OTHER
ON STAGE.
IF ONE OF
US WASN'T
ON FORM,
THE OTHER
STEPPED IN
AND TOOK
OVER.'
AGNETHA

Laughing during the filming of the 'Knowing Me, Knowing You' video

2 February The *Sun* published an article exposing alleged 'tensions' within the group. 'Secret Catfights of ABBA's Angels: It is all harmony on stage. But away from the public eye, tensions within ABBA often boil over into full-scale rows. In particular, the two girls go for each other's throats in spitting, screaming catfights.' According to the article, 'Agnetha is obsessional about being on time for rehearsals and being ready in costume on time for their stage appearances. Frida is constantly late. Agnetha, on the other hand, is not as quick on the uptake as Frida. She needs more rehearsals. She doesn't seem to grasp the musical points being made by Björn and Benny as quickly as Frida. In rehearsal, Frida's exasperation with Agnetha's slowness bubbles over and the two girls really let fly at each other.'

At the time, the group were playing in Berlin. Björn and Benny were keen to keep the article hidden from Agnetha and Frida before they went on stage. After the concert, the girls were stunned by the news. 'None of this makes sense,' said Benny, 'none of us have made any statements like this.' Björn added: 'On tour, we are together all the time. Sometimes you can get on each other's nerves and might say something you shouldn't. It would be very strange if that didn't happen. But there is no conflict within the group!' Agnetha said: 'I started crying when I read all these lies about me. Especially when I think that this all gets repeated around the world. Frida and myself have very strong personalities, but we have never come to blows. We're the best friends in the world and we tell each other everything.' Anni-Frid seemed to look at the matter with detachment and a sense of humour: 'I almost burst out laughing. Nobody could really believe that the members of a group would stay together when they're quarrelling, scratching each others' eyes out and spitting at one another!' Following the article, proceedings were taken out against the *Sun*. Afterwards, it seemed that whenever sales dropped, or if the news lacked a titillating story, the British and international press would dust off this story and use it again. Of the four members of the group, it was Agnetha who was ultimately most affected by all these remarks.

The German fans couldn't wait for the tour to reach their country. Polydor made the most of the situation by releasing the single 'Knowing Me, Knowing You'. This would be the seventh ABBA single to reach No. 1 in the German charts. Once again, the group decided to feature an unreleased track on the B-side: 'Happy Hawaii'. The original piano-guitar demo had a Fats Domino feel, with vocals by Björn and the title 'Why Did It Have To Be Me'. It was Benny's idea to try an arrangement with Hawaiian guitars. Stig wrote some lyrics to go with the title 'Happy Hawaii' and the vocals were given to Agnetha and Frida. Once the song was finished, the group all thought that it was too slow for the *Arrival* album. After having tried a country version entitled 'Memory Lane', they decided to go back to the first recording with Björn on vocals, and 'Why Did It Have To Be Me' was included on the new album. This is a perfect example of how Björn and Benny would work, tirelessly searching for original sounds and new arrangements, while still using their own melodies as a base. 'Happy Hawaii' was used in an Australian cartoon film series which animated some of ABBA's songs. (*The Complete Recording Sessions*, 1994.)

4 February Epic-CBS released the 'Knowing Me, Knowing You' single in Britain. Videos would be indispensable to ABBA this year, as the group were doing no television promotion. The 'Knowing Me, Knowing You' video was excellent. It seemed to correspond perfectly with the image the public had of the two couples – even if the four Swedes didn't smile quite as much as in previous clips!

13 February Vogue released 'Knowing Me, Knowing You'. In Belgium, the song shot straight up to No. 2 on 26 February and stayed in the charts for eleven weeks.

14 February ABBA performed in London at the Royal Albert Hall. At the end of the two concerts, the four Swedes were tired but happy as their dressing rooms were invaded by friends, various showbusiness people and journalists. Benny was still suffering from shock: 'I remember a moment in the middle of the Albert Hall night when I thought, "Good grief, Benny, this is you sitting here playing at the Albert Hall." For a little while, I could not believe it was me there. It was very hard for me to sit steady on my stool.' Anni-Frid added: 'I managed to control my nerves. At the end of the show, when the audience went wild, it was a real pleasure to be on stage!' Agnetha had a different impression: 'I was terribly nervous during the first show. I felt really strange and couldn't move, I couldn't calm myself down.' Björn concluded by saying: 'Some people say that London audiences are difficult. Maybe they are at first, but after that: wow!'

'WHEN PEOPLE COME TO ME AND SAY: "BUT REALLY, OWE, THEY LOOKED TERRIBLE IN THOSE COSTUMES!" I SAY, YES, BUT YOU MUST GO BACK TO THE 1970s, IT WAS FASHION!' OWE SANDSTRÖM

16 February Prince Rainier and Princess Grace of Monaco presented ABBA with the Carl Allen Award for Best Vocal Group of 1976. The ceremony took place at the Lyceum Ballroom in London.

17 February The group returned to Stockholm. Agnetha, Björn, Benny and Anni-Frid had a week to recover and to prepare for their departure for Australia.

18 February 'Knowing Me, Knowing You' was released in Sweden and in Holland, where the single would reach No. 3.

The group and their entourage spent a lot of time discussing the idea of making a documentary film about the tour. The prospect of a TV show called 'ABBA In Concert' had been abandoned, and eventually, the idea of a full-length film in 35mm Panavision was proposed. Everyone seemed enthusiastic apart from Benny, who still had bad memories of filming in Africa with the Hep Stars. Stig's main argument in favour of the film was that this would be the perfect opportunity for the many fans who hadn't had the chance to go to a concert to see ABBA on stage. Because this was now going to be a full-length film, Lasse Hallström had to bring along more equipment and increase the number of people on his team. It was the director who suggested the idea of having a mini-screenplay and using some actors in the film. (See 'Abba – The Movie' chapter.)

25 February ABBA flew from Stockholm to Sydney, via London. There was a reception organized at Stockholm's Arlanda airport before their departure. The Australian ambassador to Sweden, Lance Barnard, came along to congratulate Agnetha, Björn, Benny and Anni-Frid and to wish them well for their series of concerts in his country.

27 February In Australia, the euphoria – which had been dubbed 'ABBA-mania' by the media – had reached fever pitch. The record company were rubbing their hands with glee, as nobody had achieved better record sales or chart positions since the Beatles. The song 'Knowing Me, Knowing You' was at No. 9 in the charts and the 'I've Been Waiting For You'/'King Kong Song' single, originally released in 1975, had re-entered the Australian charts three weeks earlier. Keith Cronau, from RCA, had obtained Stig's permission to release a new edition of the *Ring Ring* album with a different sleeve. The album earned three platinum discs as a result.

Press conference in Australia

Vogue Records promotional poster

3–12 March ABBA gave eleven concerts in the main cities of Australia: Sydney, Melbourne, Adelaide and Perth. A total of 145,000 people came to see the group. This was the most important tour on the Australian continent since the Grateful Dead and the Rolling Stones.

13 March ABBA and the majority of their team returned to Stockholm. Stig had just received a telex informing him of the group's sales in South Africa and Rhodesia. *Greatest Hits* had sold more than 50,000 copies. *Arrival* was still No. 1 in the charts, having sold 25,000 copies in South Africa and 15,000 in Rhodesia.

1 April CBS in Sweden released an album entitled ABBA – *Our Way* by Nashville Train. The group was in fact made up of Roger Palm (drums), Rutger Gunnarsson (bass), Janne Lindgren (guitar) and some of the other musicians who worked with ABBA. The instrumental version of their song 'Please, Change Your Mind', was used in the opening credits of the film *Abba – The Movie*.

2 April 'Knowing Me, Knowing You' reached the top of the British charts and stayed there for five weeks.

9 April Björn and Benny's dream came true. A telex arrived, announcing that ABBA had reached No. 1 in the United States with 'Dancing Queen'. Agnetha remembers: 'We were in the office when all of a sudden we heard someone shouting: "ABBA are No. 1 in the U.S.A!" We immediately opened a bottle of champagne to celebrate the event!'

19 April ABBA shared the front page of *Expressen* with skier Ingemar Stenmark. The previous day at the newspaper's Spring Party they had been awarded the Golden Wasp (the wasp is *Expressen's* logo) for *Abba-Dabba-Dooo!!*, which the newspaper's readers had voted Best TV Programme of 1976. *Expressen* announced that the Swedish ABBA fan club now had more than 200,000 members. In Britain, figures were equally impressive, with 40,000 people having already subscribed.

26 April Atlantic released 'Knowing Me, Knowing You' in the United States. The single stayed in the American charts for fifteen weeks, peaking at No. 14.

At the beginning of May, Björn, Benny and Michael B. Tretow travelled to Los Angeles to meet Tom Hidley, whose mission was to construct ABBA's future recording studio, together with architects Michael Borowski and Jan Setterberg. The Polar Music studio was going to be built in an old Stockholm cinema, the Riverside. Meanwhile, Anni-Frid was taking part in the recording of Claes of Geijerstam's *Starlight* album at the Glen studios.

17 May Björn, Benny, Anni-Frid and some of their friends went to see the Eagles in concert at the Gröna Lund amusement park in Stockholm.

The Japanese label Discomate Records released 'Dancing Queen' as a single and chose 'Tiger' for the B-side. The single took ABBA to the top of the Japanese charts for the first time, an event which coincided with the release of the *Arrival* album in June.

28 May 'Knowing Me, Knowing You' reached No. 8 on the RTL chart. The single received frequent airplay on the main French radio stations, with the video being screened on television four times.

31 May Björn and Benny began recording ABBA's next album at the Marcus Music studio in Stockholm. The first track, entitled 'A Bit of Myself', would eventually become 'The Name of the Game'. The two musicians had to work to a very tight schedule since the album was planned for release during December, to coincide with the release of *Abba – The Movie*. At Polar Music, there was even talk of the possibility of a double album, with one of the two discs being a live recording of ABBA on stage in Australia.

The majority of June was devoted to filming additional scenes for the full-length film *Abba – The Movie*. Lasse Hallström and his team filmed these scenes in Stockholm and the surrounding area. Australian actors Robert Hughes and Tom Oliver flew over especially from Sydney.

1 June There were studio sessions for the new song 'Eagle'. Björn had given it the provisional title 'High, High'. 'The words came to me quite quickly,' he explains, 'after having read *Jonathan Livingstone Seagull*, the book by Richard Bach. People often said that the song was a homage to the group the Eagles, but that's not the case. I wrote the lyrics on Viggsö, in silence, surrounded by nature, water and space.'

2 June Anni-Frid went to see Lasse Berghagen's new show at the Gröna Lund amusement park in Stockholm. On the same day, Agnetha and Björn announced to the press that they were expecting their second child at the end of the year.

30 June The Swedish press announced that Agnetha would have to pay Danish composer Per Hviid 5000 Swedish kronor. Seven years earlier, he had accused Agnetha of plagiarizing his work in her song 'Om Tårar Vore Guld'. The compensation payment put an end to this prolonged controversy.

During the first two weeks of July, Lasse Hallström finished the filming of *Abba – The Movie*.

11 July Björn and Benny joined the Hootenanny Singers for a one-off concert at the Västervik Visfestival (Song Festival), where 1400 people came to watch Hansi Schwarz, Tony Rooth, Lars Frosterud and the two ABBA musicians.

☆ ☆ ☆ ☆

Throughout the summer, Björn and Benny alternated studio recording sessions with long periods of writing. The two musicians would spend hours searching for arrangements which would be just right for their melodies. The same applied to the lyrics, with them trying every idea and combination possible. 'We considered that the sound of the words was more important than their meaning,' Björn later commented. 'When we found a catchy hookline, we thought that the repetition was very effective!'

For the forthcoming album, however, they used this technique far less. The latest compositions had a new sound and different arrangements to their previous records. The lyrics were also more developed. They were slightly ambiguous ('Eagle', 'Move On'), or more profound ('One Man, One Woman', 'The Name of the Game'). Benny emphasizes the shift in approach: 'I find that it's easier to retain a liking for the songs that we recorded from this period onwards. The lyrics tend to be better and the melodies are stronger. "One Man, One Woman" is probably my favourite track off *The Album*, apart from "Thank You For The Music".' (*The Complete Recording Sessions*, 1994.)

In the studio, the two musicians had trouble trying to fit together the songs from the mini-musical which featured in their stage show, despite the fact that they had already been performed live on numerous occasions. However, Björn and Benny had composed 'Thank You For the Music', 'I Wonder (Departure)' and 'I'm a Marionette' specifically for the stage, with strong cabaret-style arrangements designed to reinforce the visual effect. The songs therefore had to be adapted for the record.

☆ ☆ ☆ ☆

'NINETY PER CENT OF THE SONGS SO FAR HAVE BEEN RECORDED WITH BACKING TRACKS, AND THE MOOD HAS BEEN THERE BEFORE THE LYRICS HAVE BEEN ADDED.' **BJÖRN**

'I DRAW MY INSPIRATION FROM ALL OVER THE WORLD: FROM CABARET PERFORMANCES, OLD MOVIES, EVEN FROM NATURE.'
OWE SANDSTRÖM
ABBA'S COSTUME DESIGNER

'The Girl With The Golden Hair' is based around four songs: 'Thank You For the Music', 'I Wonder (Departure)', 'I'm a Marionette' and 'Get On the Carousel'. It is all held together by a master of ceremonies who could have come straight out of *Cabaret*. The role was played by Francis Mathews, a twenty-four-year-old English actor. During the tour, he spoke to journalist Lottie Molund: 'Thomas Johansson was looking for an English-speaking actor and contacted my agent. I had just finished playing at the Welsh National Theatre in Cardiff. This is the first time that I've been on stage in front of 10,000 crazy teenagers. It's a weird feeling. It's a shame it's such a shallow story, because it would have been great to have had some real lines and a real person to play.' The other surprise in the show was an unreleased, tongue-in-cheek song called 'I Am an A', where the four members of ABBA jokingly introduced themselves.

During the show ABBA performed twenty-five songs: 'Tiger' – 'That's Me' – 'Waterloo' – 'S.O.S.' – 'Sitting In the Palmtree' – 'Money, Money, Money' – 'He Is Your Brother' – 'I Do, I Do, I Do, I Do, I Do' – 'Dum Dum Diddle' – 'When I Kissed the Teacher' – 'Knowing Me, Knowing You' – 'Rock Me' – 'I Am an A' – 'I've Been Waiting For You' – 'Mamma Mia' – 'Fernando' – 'Why Did It Have To Be Me' – 'Intermezzo No. 1' – 'Thank You For the Music' – 'I Wonder (Departure)' – 'I'm a Marionette' – 'Get On the Carousel' – 'So Long'. Encore: 'Dancing Queen' – 'Thank You For the Music'.

The musicians were:
Keyboards: Anders Eljas, Wojciech Ernest.
Guitars: Finn Sjöberg, Lasse Wellander.
Bass: Rutger Gunnarsson.
Drums: Ola Brunkert.
Percussion: Malando Gassama.
Sax and flute: Lars O. Carlsson.
Backing vocalists: Lena Andersson, Lena-Maria Gårdenäs, Maritza Horn.
Sound engineer: Claes af Geijerstam

EUROPE
Fifty-two people were employed by ABBA for the seventeen concerts in Europe. Thirty tons of equipment were needed for the shows.

26 January
The group arrived in Oslo during the evening. The technicians and equipment had arrived several days earlier.

27 January
Polar Music organized a reception in honour of the 150 directors and marketing people who worked for ABBA around the world. They had all been invited to the first concert of the tour. They were also here to present the group with various awards. During the day, Anni-Frid and Benny visited the Edvard Munch museum.

28 January – Oslo, Ekebergshallen
The first concert, with an audience of 5300, including Queen Sonja and Prince Harald of Norway. After the show, the royal couple went backstage to congratulate the group and to present them with gold and platinum discs for Norwegian sales of the *Greatest Hits* and *Arrival* albums.

29 January – Gothenburg, Scandinavium
The group visited Liseberg during the afternoon. Agnetha, Björn, Benny and Anni-Frid were invited to leave their handprints and signatures in cement, as is the tradition for any stars who visit the amusement park. The prints were later cast in bronze.

Mats Olsson reviewed the concert in *Expressen*: 'Björn and Benny as writers of a musical? Why not! The audience were presented with what you might call "a pocket opera". It's a clumsy story but is ground-breaking for ABBA.

'BEING ON TOUR WAS BORING REALLY, IT'S DIFFICULT FOR PEOPLE TO UNDERSTAND THIS, BUT THEY SEE THE GLAMOROUS SIDE OF IT, PEOPLE CHEERING AND ALL OF THAT. BUT REALLY, APART FROM BEING ON STAGE FOR 2 HOURS, THE REST OF IT WAS *COMPLETELY* BORING. THAT'S WHY WE TOURED SO LITTLE.'
BJÖRN

'Why Did It Have To Be Me'

'WE ALWAYS KNEW THAT LASSE HALLSTRÖM HAD GREAT TALENT. HE WAS VERY GOOD WITH MUSIC AS WELL. AND I ALWAYS THOUGHT HE WOULD GO ON TO SOMETHING BIGGER, ABSOLUTELY.' BJÖRN

ABBA THE MOVIE

It was originally intended that *Abba – The Movie* would be a documentary about the group's tour, filmed in 16mm. The idea of a TV special was then put forward, and one of the group's two concerts at the Royal Albert Hall in London was filmed by Lasse Hallström and his team. The project eventually became a full-length film, recorded in 35mm Panavision in Australia and Sweden.

Actor Robert Hughes remembers how it all came about: 'I had heard about the audition from my agent. We were told it was only going to be a 16mm documentary showing ABBA on tour and relaxing in between shows, and the radio announcer would be a linking device. I went to the screen test and met the director Lasse Hallström. He said: "I want you to do some impromptu acting." Then it turned out they were going to do some tests in 35mm Panavision and it was pouring with rain. We went to North Sydney and in the rain I walked across the flyover of the approach to Sydney Harbour Bridge on the north side. It looked fabulous and the decision was made to shoot in Panavision and to produce a major film.'

THE PLOT
Ashley, a young DJ working for an Australian radio station, finds himself with the difficult task of interviewing the Swedish group ABBA during their Australian tour. Inexperienced and without his press pass, he finds it impossible to break through the barricade of bodyguards surrounding the group. After following ABBA from town to town, he finally meets the four 'inaccessible' stars by chance in a hotel lift. Exhausted but happy, he makes it back to the radio station just in time to broadcast his report. As it goes out on the air, ABBA are leaving Australia, at the end of their triumphant tour.

FILMING
In total, 50 hours of rushes were filmed by Lasse Hallström. Robert Hughes explains: 'It was an unlimited budget. It was crazy – we just sort of went out with cameras and did things. There was no script. Robert Caswell was supposed to write the script and he was really upset because everything was moving too fast and he didn't have time to write anything. Nothing had been written down. Lasse came up with ideas on the spot. He didn't actually tell the band members that I was an actor playing a part, so I didn't really get to talk to them until the end of the tour in Perth.'

Australia, 3–12 March 1977
Several songs were filmed at each concert. However, many clips were filmed at the Entertainment Centre in Perth, since the acoustics were better there than in the other outside stadiums. Numerous outside scenes were filmed during the daytime (airports, stadiums, press conferences, interviews with fans, street and crowd scenes).

'WE WERE SO OCCUPIED WITH DIFFERENT PROJECTS LIKE RECORDING AND TOURING AND SO THE ONLY CHANCE HE REALLY HAD TO MAKE A MOVIE WITH US WAS TO RECORD IT DURING A TOUR; IN OTHER WORDS HE HAD TO WRITE SOME KIND OF STORYLINE AROUND THE GROUP TOURING, WHICH HE DID VERY CLEVERLY. IT WAS VERY SIMPLE BUT, I THINK, ENJOYABLE.' BJÖRN

'WE WRITE A SONG THAT WE'RE PROUD OF, RECORD IT THE BEST WAY WE CAN, AND RELEASE IT BECAUSE WE THINK IT'S VERY GOOD. BUT I HAVE NO CRITERION THAT IT HAS TO BE ART.'   **BENNY**

1978

Stig and the four group members had decided to channel all their energy during 1978 into promotion of the new album and the film, as well as into writing new songs.

In the UK, Agnetha, Björn, Benny and Anni-Frid had been named Top Artists of the Year by British newspaper the *Sun*. A television crew was sent over to Stockholm to film the group at Glen studios on 10 January.

13 January   Epic-CBS released *Abba – The Album* in Britain. The album had already been certified platinum and advance orders were estimated to be worth more than £1 million. The group's British record label took a different approach to other countries, releasing the album in a gatefold sleeve with a slightly bluish background instead of a white one. The photos inside the sleeve were different, too, and the tracks which were featured in the group's film were marked with a small symbol.

The critics were harsh. *Melody Maker* said, 'This is probably ABBA's weakest album since they hit the big time', adding that the mini-musical was a 'mistake'. The review in *Rolling Stone* was slightly more constructive: 'Side two is a real attempt to do something different, and, if not everything works, the effort is still laudable.' *New Musical Express* described 'Thank You For the Music' as 'the sort of tearjerker that turns up in provincial pantomimes' and claimed that the album 'could turn out to be ABBA's least satisfactory'. Sheila Prophet wrote in *Record Mirror*: 'ABBA on record shows up all their best features – their songwriting talent, their instrumental proficiency, their ability as arrangers, their vocal precision, without uncovering their worst – their clumsy stage presence, their lack of humour and their showbiz shoddiness.'

16 January   Polydor released 'Take a Chance On Me' as a single in Germany. It entered the charts almost immediately and reached No. 3, staying in the charts for a total of twenty-five weeks. ABBA would be in Germany during February for the release of their film. A journalist from *Bravo* magazine wrote of *Abba – The Album*: 'What strikes me above all about ABBA is that they always give us honest records. Unlike other artists who lack substance, they do not fill their albums with unimportant little songs but give us strong authentic material throughout.'

At the end of January, Björn, Benny, Frida and Stig travelled to the MIDEM fair in Cannes to promote *Abba – The Movie*. Agnetha stayed in Stockholm with Christian. The three members of the group stopped off in Paris on 21 January to take part in Guy Lux's *Loto Chansons* programme. They were interviewed by the presenter and a clip of 'Take a Chance On Me' was shown. Sales of the album in France were already looking promising. Pierre Lescure wrote in *Music Media* magazine: 'Since "Waterloo", every single has sold 300,000 copies in France. The group's fantastic commercial and financial achievements are due to both their inexplicable success and a rigorous and continuous marketing technique. The magic is in the general impact of the group and their music.'

15 February   Agnetha and Björn travelled to London for the British release of *Abba – The Movie*. Benny and Anni-Frid had arrived the previous day, giving them the opportunity to spend more time in the British capital.

16 February   The premiere of the film took place at the Warner West End 2 cinema, near Leicester Square. There was a big crowd outside the cinema and the atmosphere was electric. Among the journalists, photographers and celebrities present were Pete Townshend, Keith Moon and John Entwistle from the Who, actress Connie Booth and composer Biddu. After the screening

Both: Les Rendez-Vous du Dimanche TV show, Paris

'FRIDA IS A LADY WITH ENORMOUS STYLE. EVERYONE USED TO SAY THAT AGNETHA WAS THE ONE THAT EVERYONE FANCIED, AND SHE WAS A BEAUTIFUL WOMAN. BUT I ALWAYS THOUGHT THAT FRIDA WAS JUST AS VITAL.' **TIM RICE**

of the film, there was a press conference and a reception at the Café Royal in Regent Street.

ABBA were only in the British capital for a short time. Among their various promotional activities were numerous interviews, including one with Dave Lee Travis from BBC Radio One, and a photo shoot at the Crockford Casino. One of the high points of the trip was a reception at the Lyceum Ballroom, where ABBA were presented with the Carl Allen Songwriting Award by Princess Margaret.

Abba – The Album went straight in at No. 1 in the UK on 4 February and stayed at the top spot for nine weeks; the 'Take a Chance On Me' single, which had only just been released, was already at the top of the singles chart.

The film received mixed reviews, however. ABBA were criticized for not managing to achieve 'the transition of music to the big screen', despite the fact that the film's technical quality was undeniable and its production exceptional. After all, *Abba – The Movie* was only intended as a documentary showing the group on stage during their tour.

17 February   Agnetha, Björn, Benny and Anni-Frid, who were unable to attend the German premiere of *Abba – The Movie*, had decided to promote the release of the film by taking part in a TV show called *Am Laufenden Band*, presented by Rudi Carrell. During their two-day trip to Germany, ABBA also did some photo shoots and gave a press conference. The four Swedes were presented with various awards from teenage magazines, voted for by their readers, including the silver Otto award from *Das Freizeit Magazin* and the bronze Otto from *Bravo*. On Rudi Carrell's show, ABBA performed 'Take a Chance On Me' and took part in games and interviews. Anni-Frid's father, Alfred Haase, also participated in the show.

In between promotional trips, Björn and Benny continued work on the next album. The idea of writing a musical, which had been put forward the previous year, had been abandoned for the moment. Details of chart positions for 'Take a Chance On Me' began to arrive in Stig's office: No.1 in Belgium, No. 2 in Holland, No. 8 in Spain, No. 1 in Japan and No. 12 in Australia.

During this time, Lasse Hallström filmed several videos for the new album: 'Eagle', 'Thank You For the Music' and 'One Man, One Woman'.

4 March   Agnetha and Björn presented the ABBA Prize trophy to seven-year-old Agnetha Hjort at a junior skiing competition which the group had sponsored that year. The event had been named the ABBA Prize, with the winner receiving a trophy and a cheque for 100,000 Swedish kronor.

11 March   'The Name of the Game' reached No. 12 in the United States. This was ABBA's best chart position since 'Dancing Queen'. *Abba – The Album* had been released on 24 January and was slowly climbing up the American charts.

Two weeks later, Stig travelled to the States in preparation for the release of *Abba – The Movie* and the single 'Take a Chance On Me'. ABBA's producer also finalized details with Atlantic and Scotti Brothers for a massive promotional campaign entitled 'ABBA Month'. 'By and large, the U.S. still remains for us to conquer,' admitted Stig. 'We've racked up good sales over the past few years, but we still haven't broken down the heaviest doors, so to speak. To be frank, we're not the household name over there we'd like to be.'

In the middle of March, the four members of the group permitted themselves a week's holiday, Björn and Agnetha deciding to stay in Sweden, while Benny and Anni-Frid went on a skiing holiday in Austria.

3 April   A team from German pop magazine *Bravo* arrived in Stockholm. Photographer Wolfgang 'Bubi' Heilemann had reserved a studio for an extended photo shoot with the group. The mood was relaxed, despite the fact that Agnetha was suffering with flu. ABBA wore the new costumes which had been created by Owe Sandström – silk tunics with painted animals on them – as well as some of their stage clothes from the 1977 tour.

12 April   Agnetha, Björn, Benny and Anni-Frid travelled to Paris for several days of promotional work. On the first evening, they recorded the show *Les Rendez-Vous du Dimanche* in Studio 11 at Buttes-Chaumont. Michel Drucker dedicated half his programme to the group and the release of their film, entitled *Vive Abba* in France. He interviewed the group and showed some clips from the film. ABBA also performed 'Take a Chance On Me' in the studio, although this version was slightly different to the single – it had an acapella ending. The programme was screened on Sunday 16 April.

During their stay in Paris, ABBA met the press, posed for photographers and also took part in Jean-Loup Lafont's radio show, *Basket*, on Europe 1. The group were presented with a Golden Basket award by the host in recognition of their excellent score on the programme the previous year.

In the middle of April, the Swedish Tourist Office launched a massive campaign to promote Sweden overseas. Two different posters were printed, one featuring ABBA ('ABBA welcome you to Sweden') and the other featuring the Swedish Royal Family. Bertil Harrysson, director-general of the Swedish Tourist Office, explained: 'The posters and brochures we have had printed are going to be distributed all over Europe. We wanted to portray a modern image of Sweden. ABBA very kindly agreed to take part in the campaign. It also served as good publicity for the group.'

At the end of April, the four members of ABBA agreed to be interviewed by Mats Olsson for a feature in *Expressen*. Each member of the group was more candid than usual, really opening up to the interviewer, as the following extracts demonstrate:

Frida: 'Sometimes I get tired of ABBA. But then I think about it and realize that ABBA is what I do best. I want to be prepared for the future. I don't know what I'll do. For the time being I'm carrying on with taking singing and dancing lessons. I'd like to do another solo album but it's hard to find good songs. Besides, I'd like Benny to produce it and he doesn't have the time. I've had enough of the negative climate in Sweden. Especially as far as showbusiness is concerned. People seem to be more open outside Sweden, which is very stimulating. When I get back here I get very frustrated by this negative attitude.'

Benny: 'Swedish folk music and Elvis Presley are where my real musical roots lie. As long as we enjoy working together as ABBA, then we will carry on. The writing gets harder and harder. It's easy to find ideas in the beginning but the rest of it is hard. Maybe we expect too much of ourselves. If I had the time, I'd like to produce other artists. My big dream is to produce John Lennon. I have no idea of what would come out of that or even of what I would do, but in my opinion he is the greatest rock singer in the world. And as regards writing a musical, we're not ready yet and we don't have the time.'

Agnetha: 'I think that Björn would like four or five children. But I said: no more. I had a difficult pregnancy. I almost lost Christian during the seventh month. I don't know if it's my age but I've started to question myself. Time is going by so fast. I'll soon be thirty. On a positive note, ABBA has given me my independence. I come from an unassuming family. Four of us would sleep in the same room. On the negative side of things, I don't like people thinking of me as a part of ABBA instead of for the person that I am and I also find our nice image embarrassing. The media created that. We're ordinary people. We can be just as bad as anyone else. The interest in my bottom in Australia and Britain is ridiculous. I didn't realize they were filming my backside so much. On stage, we like what we wear. Benny often has ample clothes to hide his … um … chubbiness, while Frida and myself think it's nice to wear things which show off our femininity.'

Björn: 'Even if ABBA were to split up, Benny and I would carry on working together. I sometimes feel out of it in Sweden. But at the same time, Agnetha and myself are very family-orientated. We couldn't leave our parents and friends here in Sweden. We don't feel any pressure to release an album a year. We do one when we have something ready. If we're satisfied with it, then we release it. And we're delighted when it sells well. I get very angry when the newspapers write more about what we earn than our music. I agree that we earn a lot of money but we also pay a lot of tax. But they rarely write that.'

'THE OPENING OF THE POLAR STUDIOS CHANGED A LOT IN OUR WORK. IT WAS MADE TO OUR SPECIFICATIONS. IT CONTAINED ALL THE THINGS WE NEEDED, AND WE COULD GET HOLD OF THEM FAST, SO WE COULD WORK MUCH MORE SMOOTHLY THAN WE DID BEFORE, IN OTHER STUDIOS. SO, IT WAS VERY EASY TO RECORD THERE. WE HAD THE BEST EQUIPMENT IN TOWN, AT THAT TIME. IT'S STILL A GREAT STUDIO!'
MICHAEL B. TRETOW ABBA'S SOUND ENGINEER

Having fun on Olivia

30 April 'Take a Chance On Me' reached No. 8 on the RTL charts. In France, due to a lack of promotion, the film *Vive Abba* didn't do very well at the box office. It was taken off within three weeks of its release.

1 May ABBA flew to the United States. Polar Music, together with Atlantic, had invested $1 million in the ABBA Month campaign. To help matters along, Stig had also signed a contract with Scotti Brothers, who had previously promoted Barbra Streisand, John Denver and Leif Garrett. During their stay, Agnetha, Björn, Benny and Anni-Frid took part in numerous television and radio shows and met the press. *Newsweek* and *Time* magazine published extended features on the group. Special signs, posters and window displays were installed in record stores. A television and radio advert for *Abba – The Album* was also planned. On top of all this, there was also a 7-metre-high display board on Sunset Boulevard in Los Angeles.

8 May The two couples took part in Olivia Newton-John's television show. This was the high point of ABBA Month. On the programme, the group performed some of their hits and sang with Olivia and Andy Gibb. In one long sequence, the six artists did fun improvisations of various songs, ranging from the Beach Boys' 'Barbara Ann' to an operatic aria, performed by Frida. The first screening of the show was on ABC on 17 May.

Stig explained: 'Olivia said that she liked us a lot. Our participation in this programme is just the first step in a collaboration. We're going to do the same thing in September when she comes to Sweden. Polar Music are going to take care of the distribution of her records in our country.'

10 May ABBA arrived in Düsseldorf to record the TV show *Star Parade*. The group performed 'Eagle', 'Take a Chance On Me' and 'Thank You For the Music'.

Building the Polar Music studios

18 May The cream of Swedish showbusiness – artists, musicians, technicians and record-company executives – attended the opening of the Polar Music studios. Stig and his wife Gudrun greeted the guests at the entrance to the studios. Inside, Agnetha, Björn, Benny, Anni-Frid and Michael B. Tretow showed guests their new musical 'laboratory'. Built in an old cinema, the Riverside, it was one of Europe's most advanced recording studios.

7 June Vogue released the single 'Eagle'. Some countries, such as Germany, Japan and France, fearing that the song was too long to be played on the radio, had asked for a shorter version. The song was therefore cut from 5 minutes 47 seconds to 3:36. The single, which had already been released in several countries, did very well, reaching No. 2 in Belgium, No. 8 in Germany, No. 4 in Holland and No. 9 in Spain.

Promotional visit to Japan

18 October ABBA arrived in Paris for two days of promotion. During the afternoon, they went to Studio 102 at the Maison de la Radio for rehearsals of *Top Club*, a daily TV show presented by Guy Lux. The programme had very high viewing figures – it was screened just before the 8 o'clock news. Agnetha, Björn, Benny and Anni-Frid were guests of honour the following week (23–28 October). They recorded six songs in one evening, changing costumes between each filming session, and were interviewed several times by the presenter. 'Money, Money, Money' was used as the opening music. The following day, ABBA were due to sing 'Summer Night City' on a *Top Club* Special. But because of a strike by the technicians of the S.F.P. (French Production Society), the recording was cancelled. During the evening, Alain Boublil organized a dinner, in the presence of Mireille Mathieu, at the famous restaurant Le Grand Véfour. The group returned to Stockholm the following day.

25 October–10 November ABBA continued with the recording and mixing of two new tracks for the forthcoming album: 'Angeleyes' and 'If It Wasn't For the Nights'. Polar Music made an announcement to the press that the album would not be ready before spring 1979. At the end of October, Stig and Görel Johnsen travelled to Tokyo to finalize details of ABBA's pending visit to Japan.

11 November ABBA travelled from Stockholm to Los Angeles to take part in a live performance of *The Dick Clark Show* on 15 November, and to receive platinum discs recognizing sales of the albums *Greatest Hits* and *Abba – The Album* in the United States. ABBA did no promotion for 'Summer Night City', as the single had not been released in America.

16 November The group left the States and flew to Tokyo. Stig, Görel Johnsen and representatives of record label Discomate had planned ten days of promotion to consolidate ABBA's success in Japan (their previous visit had been in November 1972). Görel told the Swedish press: 'The Japanese are growing to like ABBA more and more, especially since the screening of the TV shows *Olivia* and *Studio 2*, from Poland. "Summer Night City" has just been released as a single – with a "Welcome ABBA" caption printed on it – and three albums are currently in the Top 20: *Arrival*, *Greatest Hits* and *Abba – The Album*.'

The timetable was very tight and the group had very little free time during their trip. On 20 November, ABBA gave a press conference at the Hilton in Tokyo. They took part in several radio shows and previewed a new track, 'The King Has Lost His Crown'. Agnetha, Björn, Benny and Anni-Frid also participated in several TV shows and recorded an *Abba Special*. In this hour-

ABBA TV special in Japan

long programme, the group, sometimes surrounded by dancers, performed thirteen songs – some recorded live with a backing orchestra – and unveiled the new song 'If It Wasn't For the Nights'. Japanese television made a whole feature on this ten-day promotional trip, including backstage footage from the *Abba Special*.

27 November The group landed back in Stockholm. At the end of their trip, Agnetha told *Expressen*: 'The timetable was very intense. But I have never seen such efficient people. We didn't see much of Japan apart from the hotel and the radio and TV studios. During the ten days we only had an hour and a half of free time, but we enjoyed ourselves!'

6 December The group flew to London for three days of promotion. They were accompanied by musicians Ola Brunkert (drums), Christian Veltman (bass) and Janne Schaffer (guitar). ABBA recorded two TV shows: *The Mike Yarwood Christmas Show*, on which they performed 'If It Wasn't For the Nights' and 'Thank You For the Music', and *Jim'll Fix It*, presented by Jimmy Savile. On the latter, two of the group's fans had the opportunity to meet their idols; they were chosen from 50,000 people who had written letters to the BBC. During the programme, the four members of the group announced two pieces of important news: their participation in the Unicef gala the following

January, which would take place at the United Nations building in New York, and the filming of a *Snowtime Special* the following February, a show which would be co-produced by the BBC and several other European television companies. During this brief trip to Britain, the group also attended Rod Stewart's concert in Leicester.

On their return to Stockholm, Björn and Benny shut themselves away in the studio to finish off a new track, 'Chiquitita'. It went through numerous phases before becoming the song which is so well known and loved. Originally entitled 'Kålsupare', the song quickly evolved into 'In the Arms of Rosalita' and then finally became 'Chiquitita'. From the start, it had a slightly 'dancy' feel, with castanets here and there giving the melody a Latin touch. The guitar and piano segments, as well as the lyrics, were fine-tuned until they were perfect. The two girls recorded the vocals over and over again until finally,   it was Agnetha who retained the solo parts.

Perhaps one of ABBA's real strengths was the length of time they spent in the studio. The journalists who called the group a hit-making machine would have changed their minds if they had been in the studio with them. They would have witnessed four perfectionists working until they were exhausted in order to achieve the best results possible. People close to them knew

'TO ME THE POP CHARTS REALLY HAVEN'T BEEN THE SAME SINCE ABBA'S DEMISE. IT WAS THE FIRST TIME I'D HEARD GORGEOUS HARMONIES AND ANGELIC CHORUSES THAT MADE YOU FEEL REALLY ELATED. I LOVED THE FACT THAT WHEN THEY WENT ON TO MAKE DISCO, LIKE "VOULEZ-VOUS", THEY UNDERSTOOD IT.'
ANDY BELL ERASURE

4 January Agnetha, Björn, Benny and Anni-Frid flew to New York to take part in the Music For Unicef gala to mark the beginning of the Year of the Child. Unicef (United Nations Children's Fund) is a humanitarian organization founded to help children in third-world countries. All the artists who took part in this show, which was presented by the Bee Gees, performed free of charge and all agreed to donate the rights of their songs to Unicef. Among the artists taking part were Olivia Newton-John, Earth Wind and Fire, John Denver, Rod Stewart and Donna Summer. The event was filmed on 9 January by American TV station NBC, and would be broadcast in seventy countries to an estimated audience of more than 300 million viewers. ABBA had decided to give 'Chiquitita' its worldwide premiere and this gala was obviously an excellent platform for the new song. At the end of the show, all the artists came back on stage to sing together 'He Is Your Brother'. Christina Kallum wrote in *Expressen*: 'All four members of the group – dazzling in their black stone-encrusted costumes and perched on a moveable podium in the middle of the hall – were a big success. "Chiquitita", ABBA's new song, has all the qualities of another hit and will also raise several millions for Unicef.' Curiously, Atlantic didn't release 'Chiquitita' as a single in the United States until the end of the year.

The group used their few days in the United States to meet the press and give interviews. Stig announced: 'The new album will be ready in the middle of April. I am currently in the process of negotiating a tour which will include the USA and Canada. We will give twenty-five concerts in the biggest towns of North America.'

10 January Stig and ABBA threw a party on the thirty-eighth floor of New York's Plaza Hotel, in the presence of the Swedish ambassador to the United States, Wilhelm Wachtmeister, as well as the Swedish ambassador to the United Nations, Anders Thunborg. The evening concluded at the famous Studio 54 nightclub. The following day the whole team returned to Stockholm.

16 January The Swedish newspapers ran the headline: 'ABBA Divorce: Agnetha and Björn Split'. The news came completely out of the blue. For many people it was as if a fairy tale had come to an end. The group's image of two happy couples had been shattered. In an exclusive interview with Mats Olsson in *Expressen*, Agnetha and Björn explained the situation:

Agnetha: 'What has happened only concerns the two of us. There's no point talking about what went wrong with our marriage. The fact is that Björn and myself can no longer live together.'

Björn: 'It's important to say that this is an amicable divorce, if you can call it that. In the beginning, it was all very romantic and we were in love. But after we got married, bit by bit we began to move apart. Our tastes and opinions started to differ more and more. We thought that a second child would bring us closer together.'

Agnetha: 'Christian doesn't know anything about what's going on because he's too young, but Linda understands. In the end the three of us sat down to talk about it. It's almost a month since we separated and I think she prefers to see that her two parents are happier now. And anyway, I only live 7 minutes away from Björn. The news isn't a surprise to Benny and Frida because they're close to us and can see how we work.'

Björn: 'It's not very nice to talk about all this in public. Which is why we won't be talking about our divorce any more in the future like we have done here. It's important that we stress that ABBA is not going to break up. The group means so much to us.'

On the set of *Gå På Vattnet Om Du Kan* – director Stig Björkman, Lena Nyman, Anni-Frid & Thomas Pontén

Nevertheless, despite Agnetha and Björn's declarations, the Swedish and international press continued to speculate on the reasons for their separation and the future of the group.

On the same day, the new single 'Chiquitita' was released simultaneously in Sweden and many other countries. The group's fans were doubly pleased with the single's B-side, 'Lovelight', since the song wasn't to be included on the forthcoming album.

Christer Faleij wrote in *Aftonbladet*: '"Chiquitita" is typically ABBA: the arrangement, the sound, the singing, nothing has been left to chance. Therefore, there is no surprise. When I listen to such perfection, I don't feel anything. Is this what ABBA are going to give us in the future or will Björn and Benny be able to do something new? The B-side, "Lovelight", opens with some great bars of guitar but doesn't contain any other surprises.' Mats Olsson wrote in *Expressen*: 'The song isn't bad but it's nothing unusual. ABBA had been accused of following the "disco" trend with "Summer Night City". This ballad of 5 minutes and 26 seconds is rather long to be a single. Apart from that, as usual, it's a good-quality song, well made and well produced.'

17 January Stig travelled to Cannes for the MIDEM fair. It gave him the opportunity to announce ABBA's autumn tour and to meet the representatives who were working for the group around the world.

For some time, Björn and Benny had been running short of ideas for writing and producing new songs. This bad patch was understandable: Agnetha and Björn's divorce, travelling, a busy promotional calendar and pressure to complete the new album, due for release in April – all these had obviously affected the two musicians' inspiration. It was therefore quite natural that they decided to leave the Swedish winter behind them and recharge their batteries and compose new songs in the sunshine of the Bahamas. They took off for Nassau on 22 January. Björn later announced in an interview:

'Atlantic Records suggested that we rent a house in the Bahamas. We had the chance to listen to other music there, which was very stimulating. The pleasure of writing and playing soon came back.' Several tracks first came to light there, including 'Kisses of Fire' and 'Voulez-Vous'. Björn and Benny were so pleased with the latter that they decided to record it at the Criteria studios in Miami on 1 February, together with Michael B. Tretow. The musicians from the disco group Foxy took part in the recording. Björn, Benny and Michael returned to Stockholm on 3 February.

29 January Agnetha recorded a new solo song, 'När Du Tar Mig I Din Famn' (When You Take Me In Your Arms). Agnetha – who hadn't written a song for four years – had specially composed this track for her forthcoming compilation album, *Tio År Med Agnetha* (Ten Years With Agnetha), which CBS-Cupol were going to release throughout Scandinavia. After having written an English lyric, with the title 'I'm a Fool Again You See', the singer gave the job of writing the Swedish text to Ingela Forsman.

3–5 February Anni-Frid was in Seville, Spain, for the filming of a full-length movie entitled *Gå På Vattnet Om Du Kan* (Walk On Water If You Can). The film was based on the book *Orlanda Och Världen* (Orlanda and the World). Orlanda (played by Swedish actress Lena Nyman), is a young literature student who falls in love with Anders (Thomas Pontén), a Swedish diplomat based in Argentina who is married to Anna (Anni-Frid). Although the story is based in South America, the filming took place in a wonderful villa in Seville. During a break in filming, director Stig Björkman said: 'I've been thinking about Frida for a long time. I'd seen her on television, in ABBA's videos, and I'd read some interviews. She seemed to be very intelligent and talented. She read the script and found the role serious and thought it would be interesting for her cinema début.' Frida confided: 'The fact that I was chosen came as a surprise to me. I've wanted to try something new outside ABBA for a long time. Even if I only had a small role, the first day of filming was very tough.'

'I THINK ALL FOUR OF US COULD SEE THE POTENTIAL IN THE GROUP WAS STILL THERE, SO WHY LET OUR PRIVATE LIVES RUIN SOMETHING THAT IS STILL GOOD?' BJÖRN

10 February 'Chiquitita' reached No. 2 on the British charts, where it would remain for two weeks, unable to knock Blondie's 'Heart of Glass' off the top spot. The *Daily Mirror* announced Agnetha's engagement to Swedish psychologist Håkan Lönnqvist. Agnetha responded quickly: 'Håkan is the psychologist whom Björn and myself consulted when we were having problems. Over time, he became one of our best friends. It saddens me to read all this speculation.'

14 February Agnetha, Björn, Benny and Anni-Frid took off for Leysin, Switzerland, where they were to record the TV show *Abba In Switzerland*, part of the *Snowtime Special* series being produced by the BBC. Soon after taking off from Stockholm, the plane was forced to turn back because of a technical problem caused by the bad weather. ABBA finally landed at Geneva airport an hour late. Leaving the plane, the group were invited to board a helicopter, since the BBC wanted the group to arrive in Leysin in the style of their *Arrival* album sleeve.

At 7 p.m., the group gave a press conference in the hotel's discotheque. Inevitably, questions concentrated on the divorce:

Agnetha: 'I don't want to talk about the divorce this evening. It's a private matter and we've already explained ourselves in an interview. Also, the man who has been named as my new fiancé is just one of our old friends. The only man in my life at the moment is my son Christian.'

Björn (visibly irritated): 'I assure you that Agnetha and myself work very well together but that we could no longer live together. Your questions always used to be about money. Now all you talk about is our divorce. It's a matter between Agnetha and myself. I'd be grateful if you would please stop speculating about our private lives.'

Benny: 'I can assure you that the group will carry on. Even if we were all divorced, ABBA is ABBA!'

At the end of the interview, the four Swedes were presented with a silver trophy, the *Bravo* Otto 78 (voted for by readers of the German magazine) by Thomas Heidenreich, one of the group's fans, as well as gold discs for 'Chiquitita' in the UK (650,000 copies had already been sold).

At 9 p.m., the group went to the Leysin ice rink, where the television crew filmed ABBA while they skated on the ice. Despite several falls, Agnetha, Björn, Benny and Anni-Frid enjoyed themselves and gave permission for the numerous reporters present to take photographs.

15 February ABBA mixed business and pleasure during the day's filming at the Les Diablerettes ski slopes. The group took a break for lunch and gave several interviews while sitting on the terrace of a small local café. During the afternoon, the BBC filmed them singing 'Chiquitita' in front of a snowman. This would become the official video for the song. A second version was later filmed inside the hotel and this was screened in Germany during a 1979 Christmas show.

16 February The *Abba In Switzerland* show was filmed in a big top with an audience of 2000. Even though ABBA mimed to playback tapes, they were accompanied on stage by Rutger Gunnarsson (bass), Ola Brunkert (drums) and Lasse Wellander (guitar). The group performed some of their hits and previewed four tracks from their forthcoming album: 'The King Has Lost His Crown', 'Kisses of Fire', 'Lovers (Live a Little Longer)' and 'Does Your Mother Know' (in a rockier version). The other guests on the show were Roxy Music, Ted Gärdestad and Kate Bush. *Abba In Switzerland* was screened in a number of European countries over the Easter holidays.

At this time, the BBC organized several recordings for the *Snowtime Special* series with artists like Leo Sayer, Patrick Juvet, Leif Garrett, Eruption, Bonnie Tyler and Boney M. This led the *Sun* to announce that Björn's 'new love' was none other than Liz Mitchell, one of the singers of the group Boney M. Björn denied this in *Expressen*: 'It's only a rumour. We are just friends and we talked a lot during our stay in Leysin. That's all!'

On their return to Sweden, Stig announced that this time their tour wouldn't include Australia but would concentrate on North America and Europe. 'Chiquitita' slowly climbed up the French charts, reaching No. 39 on the RTL Hit Parade. The single was breaking records in other countries: No. 1 in Belgium, No. 1 in Holland, No. 3 in Germany, No. 1 in Denmark, No. 2 in Sweden, No. 1 in Ireland, No. 1 in Spain, No. 48 in Italy, No. 3 in Japan and No. 4 in Australia.

8 March Agnetha and Anni-Frid recorded the Spanish version of 'Chiquitita'. The lyrics had been written by Buddy and Mary McCluskey, who worked for RCA in Argentina. Buddy later said: 'ABBA had been gaining popularity [here] for a long time but "Chiquitita" is what really made the break for them. The strange thing is that both versions, Spanish and English, were hits, although the Spanish one really was the biggest smash. I started helping Agnetha and Frida with their Spanish pronunciation. I went over to Stockholm and they are really very good at languages already – now their Spanish pronunciation is perfect.'

On the same evening, Agnetha, Björn, Benny, Anni-Frid, Stig Anderson and his wife Gudrun were present for the first time at the annual dinner organized by King Carl Gustav at the Royal Palace of Stockholm. Among the 160 ministers, ambassadors and other distinguished guests present was the future Swedish Prime Minister, Olof Palme.

During March, 'Chiquitita' was released in Japan. It was an almost instant hit and reached No. 3 on the charts. Since the group's visit to Japan six months earlier, the group had sold 1.5 million records there.

Voulez-Vous was chosen as the title for the new album, after a track on side one. For the sleeve, Rune Söderqvist organized a photo shoot with photographer Ola Lager. 'I haven't got good memories of this period,' says Rune. 'I had to work in a hurry. Since the album had a disco sound, we decided to take the photos inside the Alexandra discotheque in Stockholm. I then went to London to work on the artwork for the sleeve and to add some star effects and some brightness on the neon light.'

During the second half of March, Björn and Benny went back to work on the recording and mixing of the album. Two new tracks took shape: 'As Good As New' and 'I Have a Dream'. 'I remember that I was at home working on the lyrics for "I Have a Dream", and when I had finished them I rang Benny up,' says Björn. 'He and Frida were having a party, and he told me to come on over. When I got there, we ran the song through on the piano in front of the other guests, and after a while they were all singing along, because it was so easy to learn.' (The Complete Recording Sessions, 1994.)

24 March   Anni-Frid's evening was disturbed by an unpleasant incident. While she was at home with her two children, an intruder tried to get in. She told Expressen: 'The man knocked at the door and when I opened it he tried to come in. He was shouting "Can I use the phone?" I quickly slammed the door and called the police. As soon as they arrived, they took the man away for questioning.' Since no crime had been committed, he was released several hours later. The police sent someone to guard the property day and night. 'He'll keep a watch on the house until we feel safe again,' explained Anni-Frid.

5–6 April   Lasse Hallström filmed the promotional videos for the songs 'Does Your Mother Know' and 'Voulez-Vous'. A discotheque atmosphere was recreated in the Europa Films studios in Stockholm and a group of teenagers were invited along to dance around the group. Photographer Torbjörn Calvero took several hundred shots of the group during the two days of filming.

23 April   Polar Music released the Voulez-Vous album and the 'Does Your Mother Know' single simultaneously, with the other European record companies planning the releases at around the same time. In Scandinavia, 450,000 advance copies had already been ordered. Five pressing plants worked day and night to meet the album's deadline.

The lyrics of the ten songs had matured compared with those in previous albums. Stig, who had been preoccupied with business matters, had not collaborated in the writing. And if Voulez-Vous is an album with a disco feel, the famous ABBA sound was still recognizable. Björn and Benny just added a few disco ingredients (like brass and rhythm) to their arrangements. The violin sound, omnipresent in other European disco productions, especially those from Germany with Donna Summer, Boney M, Silver Convention and Penny McLean, was not to be found here. However, with the Voulez-Vous album, journalists and other music professionals still often made the mistake of referring to ABBA as a disco group. Benny explains: 'We found that disco-based rhythms suited and enhanced our music, so naturally we used them.'

Mats Olsson wrote in Expressen: 'This ABBA album is real quality. Is it better or worse than the earlier ones? I don't know. Their music is sophisticated and quite complex and a lot of the tracks need to be heard a few times before you get hooked. If you listen to "Voulez-Vous" with the volume turned right up, you realize that it's an ideal disco track. "Voulez-Vous" and "The King Has Lost His Crown" are, together with "Dancing Queen" and "Eagle", what ABBA do best.' In Vecko-Revyn, Christer Olsson wrote: 'Every song on the album could be a hit, which strikes a happy balance against the syrupy, cheap disco-sounding ballads and tasteless schmaltz which are dominating the charts around the world. ABBA are on the attack with their

'I USED TO SING ONE OR TWO TRACKS ON EACH ALBUM JUST FOR VARIETY, I SUPPOSE, AND "DOES YOUR MOTHER KNOW" HAPPENED TO BE ONE OF THOSE SONGS AND IT HAPPENED TO BE A STRONG NUMBER, SO IT WAS RELEASED AS A SINGLE.'   BJÖRN

fists full of simple, effective melodies, including disco, funk, rock and even a ballad from time to time. The songs are excellent and really catchy, full of *joie de vivre*.' And Lars Weck wrote in *Aftonbladet*: 'The track which is the best disco number, "Lovers", is, in my opinion the best one on the album, with a great heartfelt bluesy feel. After hearing a song like that and the great segments in some of the other songs, it makes you wonder what the team would come up with without the pressure and commercial constraints.' In Sweden, *Voulez-Vous* went straight into the album charts at No. 1 on 4 May. During its six months on the Swedish charts, it remained at the top spot for ten weeks.

The *Voulez-Vous* album was released on the same day in France and Belgium. To commemorate the event, Vogue decided to release a limited edition in red vinyl, as well as a picture disc. The 'Does Your Mother Know' single was No. 1 in Belgium and stayed in the charts for eleven weeks. In France, it reached No. 3 on 5 August and remained in the charts for twelve weeks.

With 'Does Your Mother Know', ABBA proved, once again, that they were always looking for new ideas for each song. The track was rockier than usual, and for the first time, Björn sang lead vocal on the A-side, with Agnetha and Frida on backing vocals. This change did not affect the record's success at all: it reached No. 4 in Britain, No. 1 in Belgium, No. 4 in Holland, No. 10 in

Germany, No. 1 in Austria, No. 1 in Finland, No. 7 in Australia, No. 27 in New Zealand and No. 9 in Zimbabwe.

3 May Agnetha, Björn, Benny and Anni-Frid took part in a demonstration in the centre of Stockholm. More than 500 artists and musicians gathered together at the Hamburger Börs to protest against the government's attempts to block the creation of an agency aimed at finding work especially for artists. At the end of this day of protest, a petition was sent to the Minister of Employment.

4 May Epic-CBS released the *Voulez-Vous* album in Britain. It was an instant hit, with advance orders of more than 400,000 copies, and had already achieved platinum-disc status. In just five weeks of sales, it would pass the million mark. Going straight in at No. 1, it stayed in the British charts for almost a year. David McCullough wrote in *Sounds* magazine: 'For ten years, the critics have been unanimous in saying that each member of ABBA is a genius.'

7 May Benny began production on the *Kom Ut, Kom Fram* album for the young Norwegian singer Finn Kalvik. Anni-Frid sang backing vocals on most of the tracks, and Agnetha and Tomas Ledin took part on the album's title track.

'Chiquitita', Musikladen, Germany

'OURS WAS WHAT YOU MIGHT DESCRIBE AS A HAPPY DIVORCE IN SO FAR AS WE BOTH AGREED THAT THIS WAS THE BEST THING TO DO. IT WAS NOT LIKE, YOU KNOW, ONE OF US HAD FOUND SOMEONE ELSE. SO, IT WASN'T AS BAD AS IT MIGHT HAVE SEEMED. THE BAD THING WAS THE KID, OF COURSE, THAT WAS THE UNHAPPY THING ABOUT IT.' BJÖRN

'WHEN AGNETHA AND I SEPARATED AND EVENTUALLY DIVORCED, I THINK PEOPLE ASSUMED THAT IT WAS BECAUSE OF THE PRESSURES OF THE BAND, BUT REALLY WE HAD DRIFTED APART AND IT WOULD HAVE HAPPENED NO MATTER WHAT OUR JOBS WERE.' BJÖRN

'I FEEL THAT ONE OF THE BIGGEST PROBLEMS IN THE WESTERN WORLD TODAY IS THE LACK OF CONFIDENCE, AND THE WAY OF LOOKING NEGATIVELY AT THE FUTURE. SO, "HAPPY NEW YEAR" IS ABOUT TRYING TO SET UP POSITIVE GOALS FOR THE FUTURE. THAT'S A POLITICAL MESSAGE IN ITSELF.' BJÖRN

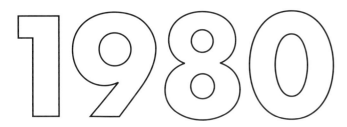

At the beginning of the year, Björn and Benny were lacking inspiration and decided to visit Barbados to compose songs for the next album. They came back with several new songs: 'Hold Me Close' (working title for 'Andante, Andante'), 'Elaine', 'Ten Tin Soldiers' (which would later become 'The Piper') and 'Happy New Year'.

On stage at Tokyo Budokan, Japan

On the plane to Barbados, Björn and Benny had the idea of writing a musical based on New Year celebrations. 'We thought it would be a good framework: a few people in a room, looking back on what has been, thinking about the future, that sort of thing,' remembers Benny (*The Complete Recording Sessions*, 1994). While staying in Barbados, they met British comedian John Cleese, and over dinner, they asked him if he would be interested in writing the story for the musical. He wasn't very enthusiastic about the idea and declined the offer. The two musicians finished writing 'Happy New Year' anyway, but abandoned the idea of the musical.

4 January   Polar Music announced that ABBA would be doing a series of eleven concerts in Japan the following March. Demand for tickets was so great that they sold out within two days of going on sale on December 16. The *Greatest Hits Vol. 2* album was currently No. 4 in the Japanese charts.

7 January   Agnetha and Anni-Frid began recording some of ABBA's hits in Spanish at the Polar Music studios. After the huge success of 'Chiquitita' and 'Estoy Soñando', the idea of recording a whole album in Spanish had been suggested, although at first Björn and Benny hadn't been too enthusiastic about the idea. Among the ten tracks which had been chosen were the obviously Spanish-sounding songs like 'Hasta Mañana', 'Fernando' and 'Move On'. Buddy McCluskey and his wife Mary had written new lyrics, and, to ensure that they pronounced the words perfectly, Agnetha and Anni-Frid called in journalist Ana Martinez del Valle to assist them. Michael B. Tretow later mixed the songs in his own studio in Sollentuna, north of Stockholm. On the new mix of 'Reina Danzante' ('Dancing Queen'), Janne Schaffer's funky guitar riffs would be more prominent than on the English-language version, where they had virtually disappeared.

At the beginning of February, on their return from Barbados, Björn and Benny immediately began recording sessions for the forthcoming album. The first few songs they worked on included 'Andante, Andante,' 'Elaine', 'The Piper', 'Happy New Year' and 'On and On and On'.

During February, the single 'Dame! Dame! Dame!' ('Gimme! Gimme! Gimme!') was released in Spanish-speaking countries. The song would stay in the Spanish charts for four weeks, peaking at No. 28.

7 February   A reception was held at the Polar Music studios to celebrate Swedish skiing-champion Ingemar Stenmark's departure for the Winter Olympic Games in Lake Placid, USA. Numerous well-known politicians and artists were present. The party continued at the Shazam nightclub with the launch of a special album entitled *Olympic Games*, featuring thirteen different Swedish artists including ABBA, Björn Skifs, Ted Gärdestad, Ann Louise Hanson, Lill Lindfors and Tomas Ledin.

24 February   The Swedish press announced that ABBA's next album would be released in October. Meanwhile, following the success of Agnetha's song 'När Du Tar Mig I Din Famn' in Sweden, an English version entitled 'Take Me In Your Arms' was planned for release in Britain, France, Germany and Holland. For some reason, however, this English version was never released.

Having triumphed over the past decade, would ABBA's success continue in the 1980s? The excellent results of the last twelve months would suggest this would be so.

Polar Music had just announced that worldwide sales of the *Super Trouper* album had exceeded seven million. This was a record in itself, as the album had only been on sale for four weeks. In Britain, with 1,700,000 copies sold, ABBA had beaten all records. *Look-In* magazine wrote: 'The key to their success must be in their ability to change with the times, without altering their basic style. Whether you love the group or hate them, you must admit that they have never made a record that has been less than technically superb.'

Elsewhere, Germany had recorded sales of 800,000 copies of *Super Trouper*, Sweden 360,000, France and Belgium 450,000, Japan 180,000, Canada 400,000 and USA 550,000. The 'Super Trouper' single achieved impressive chart positions too: No. 1 in Britain, No. 1 in Belgium, No. 1 in Germany, No. 1 in Austria, No. 8 in Spain, No. 2 in Argentina, No. 1 in Holland, No.1 in Denmark, No. 11 in Sweden and No. 1 in Finland. In Australia, the *Super Trouper* album had been given a good reception and was at No. 5 on the chart. RCA had chosen the rock track 'On and On and On' as a single (it reached No. 9 on the Australian chart) instead of the album's title track.

'I SPEND A LOT OF TIME ALONE PLAYING THE PIANO OR SYNTHESIZERS, AND IT'S MORE LIKE THERAPY: JUST TO BE PREPARED FOR WHEN IT'S REALLY ORGANIZED WORKING.' BENNY

Since 1974, sales of ABBA's singles and albums had been in the millions in the United States, Europe, Japan and Australia. They had become a pop-music phenomenon and their media coverage rivalled that of the Beatles, especially in Europe. However, in France, despite having sold more than ten million records since 1974, the group did not receive the coverage in the media that one would have expected. There was a significant reason behind this – Vogue completely lacked the desire to do any promotion. The French company relied on the success of certain records and had a tendency not to make very much effort as far as radio, TV and the press were concerned. For example, after the group's Eurovision victory, Vogue did nothing to promote ABBA in France. It wasn't until 1976 that the first articles appeared in the French press. In comparison, groups like Boney M and the Rubettes saw themselves becoming very popular in France due to the promotional efforts of their respective record companies. On the other hand, the dynamic team of Gigi Bastin and Bob Navez at Vogue Belgium worked tremendously hard to promote ABBA in Belgium. The results speak for themselves: ABBA had so far had thirteen No. 1s in the Belgian charts.

'SUCCESS REALLY CHANGES YOUR LIFE. YOU'D BE A HYPOCRITE NOT TO ADMIT THAT. THE MONEY GIVES YOU TREMENDOUS FREEDOM. I THINK THAT'S THE MOST IMPORTANT THING ABOUT MONEY.' BJÖRN

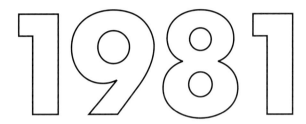

6 January Björn married Lena Källersjö in the strictest privacy, with only twelve people present. The ceremony took place in the little church at Grythyttan, in the Swedish province of Västmanland. Nobody knew about the wedding except for the couple's two families.

ABBA at Stig's fiftieth birthday party

There were no photographers or journalists present, and it was a complete contrast to the hustle surrounding Björn's marriage to Agnetha in 1971. It was a double celebration: Eva Ulvaeus, Björn's sister, had decided to marry her fiancé Alf Alsterberg at the same time. After Nils-Gustaf Sandbeck, the minister, had given the blessing, the guests were invited to a local restaurant. On the menu were soup marinière, ham and parsley with potato mousse, fillet of venison with celery purée, and French cheeses to finish. Agnetha was not present at the event. She was attending the annual ball in the winter garden of Stockholm's Grand Hotel.

On 18 and 20 January, ABBA were in the Polar Music studios to complete the recording of a song by Björn, Benny, Michael B. Tretow and Rune Söderqvist, entitled 'Hovas Vittne' (Hova's Witness). The song had been written especially for Stig Anderson, who would be celebrating his fiftieth birthday in the next few days. The group had decided to pay tribute to 'the fifth member of ABBA' with a tongue-in-cheek song. Their fans would be disappointed, because the record wouldn't be released commercially – only two hundred copies of the red-vinyl 12-inch single would be pressed. Björn and Benny recorded an instrumental version of Stig's first hit, 'Tivedshambo', for the B-side.

19 January Benny continued production on Norwegian singer Finn Kalvik's album *Natt Og Dag*, at the Polar Music studios. Agnetha, Anni-Frid, Inger Öst, Maritza Horn and Tomas Ledin sang backing vocals on some of the tracks.

24 January A TV crew filmed ABBA on stage at the Berns theatre. The group, wearing their Brighton stage clothes, performed 'Hovas Vittne'. The clip, directed by Kurt Hjelte, would be screened on 3 May 1982 on Swedish Television, on a programme entitled O.S.A. (Om Svar Anhålles – the Swedish equivalent of R.S.V.P.).

25 January Stig celebrated his fiftieth birthday. To mark the occasion, ABBA's producer had invited all his friends to his house in Djurgården. He had planned everything – apart from the many surprises which had been organized by his close friends and family. At 7 a.m., Björn and Benny climbed into his bedroom via a fire-escape ladder and began playing 'Happy Birthday Stig' on the accordion while humming along. They had just finished when a group of seven young women, dressed in cabaret costumes, came into the room and performed a special song for the occasion to the tune of 'Ljuva Sextital'. Among the dancers were Görel Hanser, Agnetha, Anni-Frid and Lillebil Ankarcrona (Rune Söderqvist's wife). An enormous buffet was waiting in the lounge later. An orchestra of fifteen musicians played at the party, welcoming guests as they arrived. More than four hundred people came to pay homage to the king of Swedish showbusiness. The event was recorded by photographers and a TV crew. After dinner, which was exclusively for Stig's close friends and family, there was a video show on a massive screen.

'WE ARE IN AN EXTREMELY PRIVILEGED POSITION BECAUSE WE CAN CHOOSE. WE ARE THE ONLY MUSICIANS IN THIS COUNTRY, AND ONE OF THE FEW GROUPS IN THE WHOLE WORLD, WHO CAN AFFORD TO DO EXACTLY WHAT WE WANT TO DO.' BENNY

'THIS WAS A VERY SAD TIME PERSONALLY, BECAUSE I SPLIT UP WITH BENNY ... WE STILL WENT ON BECAUSE WE WANTED TO FINISH *THE VISITORS* ALBUM ... WE NEVER MENTIONED IT, BUT THERE WAS A CERTAIN ATMOSPHERE BETWEEN THE FOUR OF US.' **FRIDA**

The guests had the opportunity to relive the best moments of the day and to see ABBA singing 'Hovas Vittne'. Stig was overcome when Björn and Benny presented him with the record, together with a contract signed 'Personally to Stig, for the world, for ever!'

The party was far from over, with more presents arriving and songs being sung. Before the dancing began in the evening, a mini-concert was given featuring Benny on the piano, Stig on guitar and John Spalding on drums. As a grand finale, there were fireworks lighting up the sky, spelling out the words 'Long Live Stikkan!' John Spalding remembers: 'When I decided to take Stig's dog Lucas for a walk, I found Stig, flopped out on a chair, surrounded by presents. Apparently he had just sat down, as the last guests didn't leave until 6 a.m. He had been awake for 24 hours!' A few days later, Stig thanked his friends through a mini-newspaper entitled *Stikkan-Expressen*.

During the first week of February, Björn and Benny travelled to New York. On Monday 2 February they took part in the *Tonight* show on NBC. They also met people from Atlantic, as well as American TV presenter Dick Cavett, with whom they confirmed the prospect of a *Dick Cavett Show* with ABBA. The group would make a programme with him, looking back over the past ten years with a mixture of interviews and video.

In the United States, the *Super Trouper* album had reached No. 17 in the Billboard Top 200 and had already sold more than 550,000 copies. *People* wrote: 'The ABBA sound is nasal and antiseptic. For lots of Americans, it's like marinated herring.' The rest of the trip was for their own amusement. Björn and Benny went to see three musicals: *Evita*, *42nd Street* and *Pirates of Penzance*.

From 10 February onwards, Björn and Benny continued work on the next single and the forthcoming album. During this time, Stig presented his new protégée, Kicki Moberg, to the press. Real name Kristina Elisabeth Moberg, Kicki was a nineteen-year-old girl who had sent a tape to Polar Music, and had been offered a recording contract instantly. She was given the opportunity to record a single and would also be one of the five participants in the forthcoming Melodifestivalen.

12 February The Swedish newspapers carried the headline: 'Benny and Frida divorce'. The Polar Music bulletin simply said: 'Benny Andersson and Anni-Frid Lyngstad have decided to separate. On a business level, the decision has nothing at all to do with ABBA's work.' Refusing to give any interviews, Benny only commented: 'We are conscious of the fact that the newspapers are still going to speculate, but we have to accept that. However, our personal life is our concern and no one else's. We have nothing more to add.' Polar Music made no other comment on the matter apart from

'WE FELT THAT ABBA WAS COMING TO AN END DURING THE RECORDING OF *THE VISITORS* ALBUM. BECAUSE WE WERE RUNNING OUT OF OUR ENERGY. WE WERE NOT AS AMBITIOUS ANYMORE, NOT AS COMMITTED.' **BJÖRN**

The Visitors photo shoot – Rune Söderqvist with Agnetha, Björn & Anni-Frid

'BJÖRN ASKED ME IF IT WAS SOMETIMES TOO EMOTIONAL TO SING THOSE LYRICS. BUT THAT WAS ALSO, IN A WAY, A CHALLENGE: TO BE ABLE TO PUT YOUR EMOTIONS INTO THE SONGS AND LYRICS THAT YOU SANG.' **FRIDA** ON THE SONGS WRITTEN AFTER THE DIVORCES

Frida & Claes af Geijerstam

On and On' (from November 1980) had been shown, ABBA were interviewed by satellite, live from the Polar Music studios. Björn thanked the American public and apologized for not being able to attend the event in the States, due to the distance involved and the recording of the new album. Stig Anderson, who had recently been to the USA to renew the group's contract with record company Atlantic, had brought the award back with him in his luggage.

18 August Frida and Claes af Geijerstam gave a press conference in the winter garden of Stockholm's Grand Hotel to launch *Lite Grand i Örat*. In the series of four shows, to be televised in September and October on TV2, Frida and Claes would be the presenters and would also sing, along with other guests. Frida said: 'It's fun to try to do something new. I love working in front of an audience. Unfortunately, I don't do it very often. *Lite Grand i Örat* is a programme straight from the heart. It's a bit rocky but is aimed at the whole family. There'll also be room for improvisations.' Rehearsals and filming for *Lite Grand i Örat* took place during the second two weeks of August at the Grand Hotel.

22 August Norwegian television celebrated the twenty-fifth anniversary of the Eurovision Song Contest on the programme *Momarkedet*. All the winners of the contest had been invited to come and sing their winning song in Oslo. Profits from the show would go to the Norwegian Red Cross. ABBA didn't take part in the evening. Kerstin Sehlin, from Polar Music, announced: 'The group are busy preparing their new album. Nevertheless, they won't be missing from the programme because Norwegian television came to record a message from the four members of ABBA last June.' Since the BBC had refused permission to show the Brighton clip, the Norwegian TV station decided to show ABBA singing 'Waterloo' on *Momarkedet* during the summer of 1975.

27 August Anni-Frid took part in the *Solklart* (Obvious) programme on radio station P3. She was interviewed by journalist Kjell Dabrowski, and was more open than usual in speaking about both her private and professional lives.

2 July The press announced that Frida and Claes af Geijerstam would host a series of four TV shows entitled *Lite Grand i Örat*. Claes explained: 'The idea came up last December but was delayed because of Frida's divorce. She finally accepted as soon as her problems had been sorted out. Frida has a natural charm and the ability to express herself. She is very talented.'

10 July Epic released 'Lay All Your Love On Me' / 'On and On and On' as a 12-inch single in the UK. A week later, it reached No. 7, the first time that a 12-inch single had got to such a high position in the charts. The British press seemed to have a problem accepting ABBA's continuing success. *Melody Maker* wrote: 'Over a Euro-disco backdrop, the two perfect couples weave their anthemic magic. A lovely record for Prince Charles to put on the royal turntable before consummating the wedding of all time. Lady Di should love it.'

In the United States, 'On and On and On' (which has an extra verse which was never released) did not rise any higher than No. 90 in the charts. As for 'Lay All Your Love On Me', a remixed version was a huge hit in the clubs and discotheques. Elsewhere, 'Lay All Your Love On Me' did quite well: No. 9 in France, No. 13 in Belgium and No. 26 in Germany. No videos had been filmed for these tracks; for 'Lay All Your Love On Me' a montage of old clips was created. For 'On and On and On', Anders Hanser used hundreds of photographs he had taken during the 1979 tour to create a film.

1 August Björn and Lena travelled to the Hockenheim racing circuit in Germany to give Swedish driver Tommy Slim Borgudd some encouragement before the Formula 1 Grand Prix. Tommy's car had been sponsored by ABBA.

9 August ABBA were awarded the title of Best Vocal Group of 1981 (the award covered the period 1980–81) by the American Guild of Variety Artists and the show was televised live from Las Vegas on NBC. ABBA appeared at 12.55 a.m. (9.55 a.m. European time), and after the *Show Express* clip of 'On and

29 August Lasse Hallström filmed the promotional video for 'When All Is Said and Done' at the Filmbolaget studios in Solna. The sequences in which Anni-Frid walks on the rocks were filmed in one of the islands of the Stockholm archipelago.

1–9 September ABBA were working in the Polar Music studios. Several new songs were recorded: 'Head Over Heels', 'I Let the Music Speak' and 'Should I Laugh Or Cry'. With 'Head Over Heels', Björn and Benny wanted the song to have a lively rhythm and a hidden meaning in the text. The first results were disappointing. There was a lack of humour and it was a bit heavy. Frida explains: 'Of course, our split-ups left their mark on the atmosphere in the studio. The joy that had always been present in our songs, even if the song itself was downbeat, had disappeared. We were growing apart, and the unity that had been a part of our recordings was gone.' (*The Complete Recording Sessions*, 1994.)

12 September ABBA travelled by private jet to Bournemouth, England, for the CBS sales conference. John Spalding and Judd Lander from Epic were there to welcome the four Swedes and drive them to their hotel. ABBA's attendance at the event, which the managers of CBS had kept secret, was to be the high spot of the evening. After having had some time at the hotel to recover, John, Judd and Carole Broughton (Bocu Music) drove the group to the Carlton Hotel for the cocktail party and dinner. Agnetha and Anni-Frid looked fantastic, and, for once, Björn and Benny were wearing ties. When they walked into the restaurant everyone stood up and applauded. After cocktails had been served and many speeches made, dinner began. The members of the CBS sales team were very touched by the group's presence at their annual conference, as they very rarely had the chance to meet the artists they worked for during the year. ABBA also had the opportunity to meet Jaap Eggermont, the creator of the 'Stars On 45' concept, who had had a big hit that year with his 'ABBA Medley'.

Reception at the Belfry Club, London

'THE ABBA PERIOD WAS FUN AND RESTLESS. THE SWEDES WERE ALMOST THE LAST ONES TO REALIZE HOW BIG WE WERE EVERYWHERE. BUT SWEDEN IS A BIT LIKE A DUCK-POND. WE'RE NOT USED TO THINKING BIG AND THAT'S PROBABLY WHY IT TOOK SO LONG FOR US TO GET ACCEPTED … I THINK THAT THE VERY GOOD THING WE DID FOR THE POP MARKET IS THAT WE GOT AMERICAN AND BRITISH PEOPLE TO UNDERSTAND THAT A POP SONG CAN COME FROM ANYWHERE IN THE WORLD.' **STIG**

'THE REASON OUR PROFESSIONAL RELATIONSHIP HAS ENDURED IS THAT WE ARE VERY GOOD FRIENDS WHO TRUST EACH OTHER ON EVERY LEVEL. I WAS LIKE THE BROTHER BENNY NEVER HAD, AND I SUPPOSE HE WAS THAT FOR ME TOO.' BJÖRN

1982

3 January Lena Ulvaeus gave birth to a baby daughter, who was named Emma. The baby was 50 centimetres long and weighed 3.1 kilograms.

10 January It was Benny's turn to become a father again. His wife Mona gave birth to a 2.8-kilogram boy, Ludvig, four weeks before reaching full term.

21 January Lasse Hallström filmed the video for the song 'Head Over Heels' at Svenskfilmindustri film studios in Gröndal, near Stockholm. This is certainly the group's funniest-ever video. Anni-Frid plays the leading role of a woman who rushes through her life, running in and out of stores every day in search of new outfits to wear; her husband, played by Björn, is completely exhausted.

23 January The Swedish press announced that Agnetha would be starring in director Gunnar Hellström's next film.

27 January ABBA recorded a special film clip at the Polar Music Studios, in which Björn addressed a message of solidarity to Poland. The short film would be shown on the American television programme *Let Poland Be Poland* in March.

5 February Epic released 'Head Over Heels' in Britain. The single reached No. 25 in the British charts. It was the first time since 'S.O.S.' in 1975 that an ABBA single had not reached the Top 10.

During the month of February, a Spanish TV crew travelled to Stockholm to film part of the *Aplauso* show with ABBA. The promotional videos for 'No Hay A Quien Culpar', 'Head Over Heels' and 'One of Us' were shown and the group answered questions. However, the interview wasn't one of their best, and Agnetha, Björn, Benny and Anni-Frid gave the impression that their hearts weren't really in it. They seemed indifferent, had little enthusiasm and looked unhappy. They had never been seen like this before. *The Visitors* album was No. 6 in the Spanish charts at that time and the 'Head Over Heels' single No. 18.

13 February The album *The Visitors* peaked at No. 29 in the American charts. Bill Provick wrote in the *Citizen*: 'This is a really good album with good-quality sound, production and performance. Great to listen to in every way.' In the United States, Atlantic had decided to release 'When All Is Said and Done'/'Should I Laugh Or Cry' as a single. It reached No. 27 on 13 March.

Between 15 February and 31 March, Frida was recording her solo album at the Polar Music studios. The record was produced by Phil Collins. For the duration of the recording, Phil and his musicians stayed at Stockholm's Grand Hotel. The team was made up of Mo Foster on bass, Daryl Stuermer on guitar, Peter Robinson on keyboards and Phil Collins on drums and percussion, as well as Phil's sound engineer Hugh Padgham. Choosing the songs was difficult, and Frida listened to hundreds of tracks written especially for her by numerous well-known and unknown composers.

Benny replied: 'It was in Cannes, during the MIDEM, when a journalist asked me "Do you like music?" and "How do you make a hit?"'. ABBA closed *Nöjesmaskinen* by singing a verse and the chorus of 'Thank You For the Music', accompanied by piano and guitar, and 'Under Attack', which they performed to playback. After the show, Frida served champagne to the crew.

ABBA had only 30 minutes of airtime to mark their ten years of success; Swedish Television missed the opportunity to do something to mark this anniversary. The Dutch television company Veronica did make an hour-long documentary entitled T*he Story of* ABBA. Agnetha, Björn, Benny, Anni-Frid and Stig were interviewed by journalist Annette van Trigt, speaking at length about their careers, before and during ABBA.

20 November   Stig Alkhagen wrote in E*xpressen*: 'The quartet are, in my opinion, better than ever. Their singing style has evolved considerably. Particularly Agnetha on the song "Thank You For the Music".'

Those who had predicted a commercial flop for 'The Day Before You Came' were proved wrong. The record reached No. 3 in Sweden, No. 5 in Norway, No. 32 in Britain, No. 19 in France, No. 1 in Belgium, No. 3 in Holland, No. 5 in Germany, No. 29 in Spain, No. 19 in Mexico and No. 48 in Australia.

At a private reception on the top floor of Polar Music, Stig had recently handed out a number of awards for record sales in Sweden. Each member of ABBA, as well as Michael B. Tretow, had been given a gold disc for T*he Visitors* album. There was also a gold disc for Agnetha and Tomas Ledin for their song 'Never Again'. Finally, Frida was presented with a platinum disc for the *Something's Going On* album and a gold disc for the single 'I Know …'. Overseas, the first reports of sales of her album were promising: 100,000 copies sold in Sweden, 98,000 copies in Germany and 50,000 in Canada. In France and Belgium, Vogue had sold more than 400,000 copies of the single 'I Know …'.

25 November   Frida sent a letter to the Swedish daily newspapers to announce her decision to move to London. By writing directly to the newspapers, the ABBA singer hoped to avoid any rumours or speculation which could arise after her departure from Sweden. She wrote: 'I've decided to leave Sweden. It's something that I've wanted to do for the past two years and is now going ahead. I want to protect my integrity as a private person and I also have a need for some anonymity which I can't have in Stockholm or in Sweden. My career as an international solo artist has also influenced my decision. I will be spending a great deal of my time in Britain, so London is therefore an ideal location for my activities. ABBA is not breaking up. We will carry on working together for as long as it is beneficial to us. There is no political or economic reason behind my decision to leave.' Frida had sold her Stockholm flat to Görel and Anders Hanser and had bought herself a pied-à-terre in Mayfair. Her children weren't going with her. Her son Hans, who was nineteen, was working as a sound engineer in Sweden and her daughter, Lise-Lotte, who was fifteen, was studying in the United States.

3 December   The single 'Under Attack' was released in the UK, a record very unlike ABBA's others. The B-side was an unreleased track, 'You Owe Me One'. The song was not memorable and it was arguable whether this style really suited the group. One had the impression that through lack of time or inspiration, they had thrown together the vocal arrangement and the production. They had favoured an electronic sound and technique to the detriment of originality.

On the same day, Anni-Frid took part in the programme *Nöjesmagasinet* on Radio P3. She was interviewed by journalist Kjell Dabrowski and talked about leaving Sweden.

Strangely, the 'Under Attack' single wasn't released at the same time everywhere. It was released in January 1983 in France and Australia, while

Polar Music didn't release it in Scandinavia until 21 February. The single's chart positions were mixed: No. 26 in Britain, No. 1 in Belgium, No. 5 in Holland, No. 9 in Germany and No. 96 in Australia (in February 1983). 'Under Attack' didn't chart in Sweden or Norway. It reached No. 19 in France in May 1983.

11 December ABBA appeared on Noel Edmonds' Late, Late Breakfast Show in Britain via a live link from a TV studio in Stockholm. They performed 'I Have a Dream', surrounded by children. This was ABBA's final exclusive performance of the year, and afterwards Noel asked them some rather banal questions: 'What's your favourite animal?', 'What was the most boring film you ever saw?' and 'What were your worst holidays?' It's easy to understand why Agnetha, Björn, Benny and Anni-Frid seemed uninspired by this interview. The four Swedes concluded their appearance on the show with 'Under Attack'. After the cameras had stopped rolling, the group were presented with the Expressen Spelmannen Prize for Best Musicians of 1982. According to Hans Åstrand, from the Swedish Academy of Music, 'What motivated the jury's choice was ABBA's professionalism more than anything else. It seems that there's no room for improvisation in the ABBA sound.'

With The Singles – The First Ten Years, the final chapter in an extraordinary success story was coming to an end. The group's worldwide sales were estimated at 175 million in 1982; no other group since the Beatles has surpassed ABBA's achievement. In Britain alone, ABBA sold more than 18 million records in eight years, a real achievement in a country considered the world leader in pop music, and where it was almost impossible at that time for a foreign artist to break through.

Agnetha, Björn, Benny and Anni-Frid talked about having a long break from ABBA to work on their individual projects. Agnetha was preparing her solo album with producer Mike Chapman. Anni-Frid wanted to record a new album, too, while Björn and Benny were still having discussions with Tim Rice about writing a musical.

But was it a break or a separation? No one could answer that question – not even the four members of ABBA themselves. During their career, they had often said: 'ABBA will carry on as long as we enjoy working together. The day that we are tired of it, we'll stop.' That day had perhaps arrived, but nobody dared admit it. For more than a year, there had been a certain sense of weariness, which manifested itself through a general feeling of gloom. The magic had gone. One should not forget that the strength and the balance within ABBA was, before anything else, derived from the fact that the two couples were together constantly both on stage and off. Benny and Anni-Frid's divorce only escalated the crisis which had begun when Björn and Agnetha had separated in 1979. Despite the tensions, everyone tried to keep the flame alive. But their hearts were no longer in it. The four Swedes were no longer all looking in the same direction.

In her book As I Am, Agnetha described the situation very well: 'We had reached a dividing line. We felt pretty tired of ABBA and everything surrounding it. It was time for all of us to go our separate ways, so that we could grow. It was a natural progression. Was it just a temporary break? Would ABBA ever make a new record together? We couldn't answer the questions ourselves, because none of us knew. Whether our paths crossed again depended on how we all developed. Perhaps, in the back of our minds, we thought that if Björn and Benny did any suitable songs we might work together again.'

The group's last official TV appearance took place on 18 January 1986. Agnetha, Björn, Benny and Anni-Frid sang 'Tivedshambo' on a programme paying homage to Stig Anderson, entitled Här Är Ditt Liv (This Is Your Life). The clip was filmed during the afternoon of 16 January in Benny's work room, on the top floor of the Polar Music building. Görel Hanser organized everything in secret while Stig was away. Benny played the accordion, Björn

'I CAN'T IMAGINE ANY OTHER GROUP BETTER TO WORK WITH BECAUSE THEY WERE ALL EASY-GOING. THE ONLY THING I CAN COMPLAIN ABOUT IS THAT WE NEVER GOT ANY LUNCH AND I WAS HUNGRY FOR TEN YEARS. WHEN I ALMOST FAINTED AND THERE WERE RED MISTS BEFORE MY EYES, THEN THEY SAID, "OK, LET'S BREAK FOR LUNCH!"' MICHAEL B. TRETOW

was on guitar and Anni-Frid and Agnetha read the lyrics from a huge board held up by Görel. At the end of the filming, which lasted an hour, Anni-Frid went back home to Switzerland. Björn and Benny were present for the live screening of *Här Är Ditt Liv* from the Malmö TV studios.

☆ ☆ ☆ ☆

ABBA'S PROMOTIONAL VISITS TO BRITAIN AND GERMANY

For the release of the double compilation album *The Singles – The First Ten Years*, ABBA had planned two important visits to Britain and Germany.

Wednesday 3 November
Agnetha arrived at Heathrow Airport at 3 p.m. After checking in at the Dorchester Hotel, she went to do some Christmas shopping in town. At 8 p.m. she met up with Carole Broughton from Bocu Music who took her for dinner at the Polynesian restaurant Trader Vic, one of Agnetha's favourite places.

Frida arrived at 11 p.m. from New York by Concorde.

Thursday 4 November
Björn and Benny arrived at the hotel at 6 p.m. Before giving several interviews, Agnetha, Björn, Benny, Frida and their entourage went to a secret location for dinner.

Friday 5 November
ABBA arrived at the Park Lane Hotel at 11.30 a.m. for a photo shoot. It was pandemonium and the dining room was unable to contain the crowd. The atmosphere was hysterical. Order was restored when someone decided to organize two separate photo shoots – one for the weekly press and another for the daily newspapers. It was very hot in the room but, despite the non-stop camera flashes, the group carried on smiling.

At 2 p.m., two limousines drove ABBA to the Belfry Club. A reception for the music industry and the press had been organized by Epic to celebrate the group's ten years together. On their arrival, the police had to help Agnetha, Björn and Benny to get through the crowd and inside the club. Meanwhile, Frida, who had got separated from the rest of the group, spoke with fans and signed autographs on the pavement in front of the building. Maurice Oberstein, the president of CBS, gave a speech and presented ABBA with a huge frame containing twenty-three gold discs. After lunch, a massive cake was brought in, complete with ten candles. Agnetha spent a long time talking to her future producer, Mike Chapman.

At 9.30 p.m., Agnetha, Björn, Benny, Stig, Görel, Anders Hanser, Judd Lander (ex-Epic), John Spalding and Carole Broughton went on to a restaurant on the Fulham Road, September's. Frida did not join them.

Saturday 6 November
At 11.15 a.m., Benny and Agnetha arrived at the BBC studios to record the programme *Saturday Superstore*. The two members of ABBA did not seem very relaxed in front of the cameras. Meanwhile, Björn and Frida were giving more interviews at the Dorchester Hotel and were appearing on the radio show *Junior Choice*.

At 3.30 p.m., ABBA were at rehearsals for the TV programme *The Late, Late Breakfast Show*, presented by Noel Edmonds. Several hundred fans were in the studio audience.

The programme was screened live at 6.45 p.m. The group's appearance on the show began with the promotional video for 'The Day Before You Came'. Noel then asked the group questions in between clips from the group's different promotional videos. At the end of the show, Agnetha and Frida sang 'Thank You For the Music', accompanied by Benny on piano and Björn on guitar.

At 10 p.m., the group dined at La Nassa, an Italian restaurant in Chelsea. Tim Rice and his wife joined them there, as well as Helen, Benny's daughter.

Sunday 7 November
ABBA left London for Germany. The group stayed at the Kongress Hotel in Sarrebrück. During their stay, the group gave many interviews, including one for *Tommy's Pop Show*, and did some photo shoots. Polydor held an important reception in their honour.

Monday 8 November
Agnetha and Tomas Ledin travelled to Bremen for the recording of the television show *Musikladen*.

Wednesday 10 November
Dress rehearsal for the TV programme *Show Express* at the Saarlandhalle in Sarrebrück, at 7.30 p.m. Numerous French fans had travelled from Paris to be in the audience.

Thursday 11 November
At 7.30 p.m., *Show Express* was transmitted live, with a studio audience of 2000. Amid fierce applause, presenter Michael Schanze introduced ABBA. Encircled by smoke and standing alone in front of a huge ABBA logo, Agnetha began singing 'The Day Before You Came'. The set began to revolve, revealing the rest of the group, with Frida sitting on a white piano. The atmosphere was electric. After 'Cassandra', ABBA performed 'Under Attack'. The show finished with the crowd going wild and fans storming the stage.

☆ ☆ ☆ ☆

' "THE DAY BEFORE YOU CAME" WAS VERY EMOTIONAL, BECAUSE THAT WAS THE LAST ABBA SONG WE EVER DID, AND IT SORT OF FELT LIKE "NOW IT'S OVER".'
MICHAEL B. TRETOW

'ABBA NEVER OFFICIALLY BROKE UP. IN 1982, WE JUST SAID WE WERE GOING TO HAVE A REST AND THAT WAS IT.' **BJÖRN**

'BJÖRN AND I WANTED TO WORK TOGETHER ON A MUSICAL PROJECT. THIS WAS ACTUALLY WHY WE TOOK A BREAK FROM ABBA. WE NEVER REALLY SAID WE WOULD QUIT, BUT THAT IS WHAT HAPPENED, AND I THINK IT WAS THE RIGHT THING TO DO.' **BENNY**

'THEY WERE THE ONLY GROUP THAT SET MY SPINE TINGLING. THEY MADE GREAT POP TUNES THAT HAVE STOOD THE TEST OF TIME.' **ANDY BELL** ERASURE

WHERE ARE THEY NOW?

Agnetha Fältskog

Following the success of ABBA Agnetha released three solo albums *Wrap Your Arms Around Me* (1985), *Eyes of a Woman* (1987) and *I Stand Alone* (1987), as well as an album with her son Christian, *Kom Föli Med I Vår Karusell*. In 1990, she married surgeon Tomas Sonnenfield, but they divorced two years later. She also became the victim of a stalker, her ex-boyfriend Gert van der Graaf. This incident and the demands of fame caused her to retreat far from the public gaze to the Swedish island of Ekero, near Stockholm.

For a long time, Agnetha remained a recluse. Agnetha was treated badly by journalists, and one can understand why, for reasons of self protection, she severed all contact with the media. To the disappointment of her fans she declined all interviews, earning her the title, 'the new Greta Garbo'.

In 1996 she published a memoir, *As I Am*, followed by a compilation of her songs, *My Love, My Life*. After this, she once more retreated to self imposed isolation.

However, at the age of 53, Agnetha recently made a comeback. In 2004 she released *My Colouring Book*, a compilation of her old favourites, such as 'If I thought you'd Ever Change Your Mind' and 'Sometimes When I'm Dreaming' to huge success and great critical acclaim. Agnetha is still wary of the media, though, and took only a low key role in the promotion of her new album. Despite this, *My Colouring Book* sold half a million copies worldwide.

Whether this signals the beginning of a new chapter for Agnetha is yet to be seen, but there are rumours she may be recording a new album.

'I AM NOW DOING WHAT I ALWAYS WANTED TO DO, WRITING SONGS, SINGING, AND RECORDING, AND BEING A LITTLE STAR. I LIKE BEING A LITTLE STAR, BEING A BIG STAR IS TOO MUCH PRESSURE AND I DON'T LIKE PRESSURE AT ALL.' **AGNETHA**

'I THINK IT'S SO PATHETIC WHEN OLD BANDS WHO HAVE BROKEN UP GO ON THE ROAD AGAIN. I THINK IF WE DID, IT WOULD BE A DISAPPOINTMENT TO EVERYONE. IT WOULD TAKE AWAY THE CHARISMA.' BJÖRN

Björn Ulvaeus

From 1984 to 1990, Björn resided in England with his wife, music journalist Lena, and their daughters Emma and Anna, where he founded an IT business with his brother. They have now returned to Sweden and currently live contentedly in Stockholm.

Since 1966, his collaboration with Benny Anderson has been almost constant. The two musicians have worked together on *Chess* (1984) with Tim Rice, and *Kristina Från Duvemåla*, based on the novel *Utvandrarna* (The Emmigrants) by Vilhelm Moberg, an epic saga of Swedish emigrants to the United States in the nineteenth century. *Kristina Från Duvemåla* was an unparalleled triumph in Sweden.

Björn and Benny have recently had huge success with their biggest major project since ABBA, *Mamma Mia*, the hit musical based on classic ABBA songs. Opening in 1999 in London, England, the show has toured the United States after opening on Broadway, and played to enraptured audiences in Toronto, Melbourne, Hamburg and Tokyo.

Björn also devotes much of his time to human rights and other humanist issues, as an active member of *Humanistera*, the International Humanist and Ethical Union's Swedish member organisation. In 2006, he was awarded their annual prize, *Hedenius-priset*.

Benny Andersson

Since ABBA Benny has pursued an active musical career. As well as collaborating with Björn on *Mamma Mia* and *Kristina Från Duvemåla* Benny has developed his love of folk music. He has released three instrumental Swedish solo albums and given numerous concerts in Sweden with his band, *Benny Andersons Orkestor*.

Benny also composes songs for stage and screen, and has even worked on an official Swedish hymn. Following the success of *Kristina Från Duvemåla* Benny is one of the most respected composers in Sweden. With Björn he received a Special International Ivor Novello award, and he was also given an honorary professorship in 2002 by the Swedish government for his 'ability to create high class music reaching people around the world'. He has served on the committee in charge of the Stockholm Royal Opera, and received four Swedish Grammis awards.

Benny and his wife Mona divide their time between Stockholm and his second home in the south of Sweden. His other passions include racing horses and collecting works of art, as well as producing new talent on his Mono Music label.

'TALK OF A REVIVAL IS SILLY IN A SENSE BECAUSE ABBA HAVE REACHED THAT STAGE WHERE THEIR SONGS ARE CLASSICS. JUST AS THE BEATLES HAVE LIVED FOR YEARS, EQUALLY ABBA ARE STILL GOING TO GO ON AND ON AND ON.' STEVE REDMOND EDITOR, *MUSIC WEEK*

'ABBA HAS MEANT VERY MUCH TO ME, AND STILL DOES BECAUSE IT'S NOT SOMETHING YOU JUST HANG UP LIKE A COAT. ABBA IS A VERY BIG PART OF MY LIFE, ESPECIALLY SINCE THERE'S BEEN THIS REVIVAL.' FRIDA

Anni-Frid Lyngstad

During the 1980s, Anni- Frid lived in London and Paris. Having taken part in a French musical entitled *Abbacadabra*, she recorded a second solo album, *Shine*, in 1984, and took part in several musical projects.

Anna-Frid then chose to retire from the music scene in order to devote all her time to her new passion: the environment. In order to raise funds for her *Artister För Miljö- Det Naturliga Steget* association, she returned to the stage again in 1992 for a one-off concert at the Royal Palace of Stockholm, together with other artists. She didn't feel at all out of place in this setting – she has been a great friend of Queen Silvia's for many years and had herself married Prince Ruzzo Reuss von Plauen, a childhood friend of King Carl Gustaf XVI.

In 1996, Frida made a dazzling return to music with the Swedish-language album *Djupa Andetag*. It was an enormous success, reaching No. 1 in the Swedish charts, but the album's release was limited to Scandinavia. The hectic pace of the ABBA years no longer suited her; she wished to retain the balance and harmony she had achieved after Abba.

However, life has been difficult for Frida. In 1998, her daughter Lise-Lotte was killed in a car accident, and Prince Ruzzo died the next year after a long illness.

In May 2002, she recorded a duet with Italian opera singer Fillipa Giordano: 'La Bacarolle', from Offenbach's *The Tales of Hoffman*, and in 2004 a song written for her by Deep Purple's Jon Lord, with the hopeful title, 'The Sun Will Shine Again'. Today, Frida leads a quiet life in Switzerland, devoting most of her time to charity and environmental issues.

Stig Anderson

At the beginning of the 1980s, Stig was one of the richest men in Sweden. However, he was to lose a great deal of money through bad investments. His relations with the members of ABBA became distant, with the exception of Frida, to whom he remained close. In 1989, he sold Polar Music and Sweden Music Publishing to Polygram. Several years later, he created the Polar Music Prize, the musicians' equivalent of the Nobel Prize.

Stig died of a heart attack on 12 September 1997. Björn said in his tribute: 'Stig Anderson meant a lot to me both as a human being and as a mentor.' Stig had written more than 3000 songs.

ABBA – The Museum

Plans are currently being finalised for an ABBA Museum, set to open in 2009. The site for the museum is an old customs warehouse in Stockholm. The building will house an interactive exhibition celebrating ABBA's music and their time in the spotlight, filled with images of ABBA and original ABBA costumes and instruments. Björn, Benny, Agnetha and Anni-Frid have all given their blessing and contributed items for display, and so the museum will be a true monument to the band's success story.

'I'M VERY HAPPY BECAUSE THE ABBA REVIVAL SHOWS THAT OUR MUSIC IS STILL OUTSTANDING. AND THIS HAD TO BE PROVED, BECAUSE WE HAD SO MANY CRITICAL VOICES DURING THE TIME THAT WE WERE WORKING ACTIVELY. SO THIS IS A KIND OF STATEMENT THAT WE REALLY MADE IT.' FRIDA

1973 (March)

RING RING

Ring Ring (Swedish version), Another Town Another Train, Disillusion, People Need Love, I Saw It In the Mirror, Nina Pretty Ballerina, Love Isn't Easy (But It Sure Is Hard Enough), Me and Bobby and Bobby's Brother, He Is Your Brother, Ring Ring (English version), I Am Just a Girl, Rock 'n' Roll Band

Remastered CD (2001)

+ She's My Kind of Girl, Merry-Go-Round, Santa Rosa

1974 (March)

WATERLOO

Waterloo (Swedish version), Sitting In the Palmtree, King Kong Song, Hasta Mañana, My Mama Said, Dance (While the Music Still Goes On), Honey Honey, Watch Out, What About Livingstone, Gonna Sing You My Lovesong, Suzy-Hang-Around, Waterloo (English version)

Remastered CD (2001)

+ Ring Ring (1974 US remix), Honey Honey (Swedish version)

1975 (April)

ABBA

Mamma Mia, Hey Hey Helen, Tropical Loveland, S.O.S., Man In the Middle, Bang-a-Boomerang, I Do I Do I Do I Do I Do, Rock Me, Intermezzo No.1, I've Been Waiting For You, So Long

Remastered CD (2001)

+ Crazy World, Medley: Pick a Bale of Cotton/ On Top of Old Smokey/Midnight Special

1975 (November)

GREATEST HITS

S.O.S., He Is Your Brother, Ring Ring, Hasta Mañana, Nina Pretty Ballerina, Honey Honey, So Long, I Do I Do I Do I Do I Do, People Need Love, Bang-a-Boomerang, Another Town Another Train, Mamma Mia, Dance (While the Music Still Goes On), Waterloo

N.B.

Fernando was included on later pressings

1976 (October)

ARRIVAL

When I Kissed the Teacher, Dancing Queen, My Love My Life, Dum Dum Diddle, Knowing Me Knowing You, Money Money Money, That's Me, Why Did It Have to Be Me, Tiger, Arrival

Remastered CD (2001)

+ Fernando, Happy Hawaii

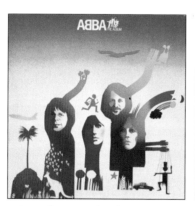

1977 (December)

ABBA – THE ALBUM

Eagle, Take a Chance On Me, One Man One Woman, The Name of the Game, Move On, Hole In Your Soul, The Girl With the Golden Hair: Thank You For the Music/I Wonder (Departure)/I'm a Marionette

Remastered CD (2001)

+ Thank You For the Music (Doris Day version)

1979 (April)

VOULEZ-VOUS

As Good As New, Voulez-Vous, I Have a Dream, Angeleyes, The King Has Lost His Crown, Does Your Mother Know, If It Wasn't For the Nights, Lovers (Live a Little Longer), Kisses of Fire

Remastered CD (2001)

+ Summer Night City, Lovelight, Gimme! Gimme! Gimme! (A Man After Midnight)

1979 (October)

GREATEST HITS VOLUME 2

Gimme! Gimme! Gimme! (A Man After Midnight), Knowing Me Knowing You, Take a Chance On Me, Money Money Money, Rock Me, Eagle, Angeleyes, Dancing Queen, Does Your Mother Know, Chiquitita, Summer Night City, I Wonder (Departure), The Name of the Game, Thank You For the Music

CD version (1983)

No bonus tracks

1980 (June)

GRACIAS POR LA MUSICA

Gracias Por La Musica, Reina Danzante, Al Andar, Dame! Dame! Dame!, Fernando, Estoy Soñando, Mamma Mia, Hasta Mañana, Conociéndome Conociéndote, Chiquitita

Remastered CD version:
ABBA Oro (2002)

Fernando, Chiquitita, Gracias Por La Musica, La Reina Del Baile (new title for Reina Danzante), Al Andar, Dame! Dame! Dame!, Estoy Soñando, Mamma Mia, Hasta Mañana, Conociéndome Conociéndote, Felicidad, Andante Andante, Se Me Esta Escapando, No Hay A Quien Culpar, Ring Ring

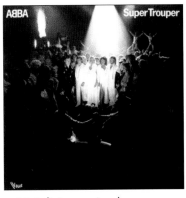

1980 (November)

SUPER TROUPER

Super Trouper, The Winner Takes It All, On and On and On, Andante Andante, Me and I, Happy New Year, Our Last Summer, The Piper, Lay All Your Love On Me, The Way Old Friends Do

Remastered CD (2001)

+ Elaine, Put On Your White Sombrero

1981 (November)

THE VISITORS

The Visitors, Head Over Heels, When All Is Said and Done, Soldiers, I Let the Music Speak, One of Us, Two For the Price of One, Slipping Through My Fingers, Like an Angel Passing Through My Room

Remastered CD (2001)

+ Should I Laugh Or Cry, The Day Before You Came, Cassandra, Under Attack

1982 (November)

THE SINGLES – THE FIRST TEN YEARS

Ring Ring, Waterloo, So Long, I Do I Do I Do I Do I Do, S.O.S., Mamma Mia, Fernando, Dancing Queen, Money Money Money, Knowing Me Knowing You, The Name of the Game, Take a Chance On Me, Summer Night City, Chiquitita, Does Your Mother Know, Voulez-Vous, Gimme! Gimme! Gimme! (A Man After Midnight), I Have a Dream, The Winner Takes It All, Super Trouper, One of Us, The Day Before You Came, Under Attack

CD version (1983)
No bonus tracks

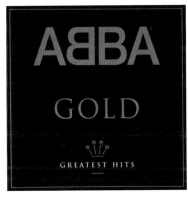

1992 (September)

ABBA GOLD

Dancing Queen, Knowing Me Knowing You, Take a Chance On Me, Mamma Mia, Lay All Your Love On Me, Super Trouper, I Have a Dream, The Winner Takes It All, Money Money Money, S.O.S., Chiquitita, Fernando, Voulez-Vous, Gimme! Gimme! Gimme! (A Man After Midnight), Does Your Mother Know, One of Us, The Name of the Game, Thank You For the Music, Waterloo

Reissued CD (2002)
Revised booklet and updated liner notes

1994 (October)

THANK YOU FOR THE MUSIC

4 CD box set containing 66 singles and album tracks and featuring:
– 6 unreleased tracks
– 6 on CD for the first time
– unreleased studio sessions including 'Just Like That'
– 68-page booklet with rare photographs, memorabilia and full cover notes

2001 (October)

THE DEFINITIVE COLLECTION

People Need Love, He Is Your Brother, Ring Ring, Love Isn't Easy (But It Sure Is Hard Enough), Waterloo, Honey Honey, So Long, I Do I Do I Do I Do I Do, S.O.S., Mamma Mia, Fernando, Dancing Queen, Money Money Money, Knowing Me Knowing You, The Name of the Game, Take a Chance On Me, Eagle, Summer Night City, Chiquitita, Does Your Mother Know, Voulez-Vous, Angeleyes, Gimme! Gimme! Gimme! (A Man After Midnight), I Have a Dream, The Winner Takes It All, Super Trouper, On and On and On, Lay All Your Love On Me, One of Us, When All Is Said and Done, Head Over Heels, The Visitors (Crackin' Up), The Day Before You Came, Under Attack, Thank You For the Music

Bonus tracks
Ring Ring (1974 remix, single version), Voulez-Vous (1979 extended remix)

Agnetha, Björn, Benny, Frida Fan Club
P.O. Box 3079, 4700 GB Roosendaal
The Netherlands
e-mail: abba@concepts.nl
website: http://abba.muziek.net

'ABBA'S HITS ARE SO MUCH BETTER THAN ANYONE THOUGHT AT THE TIME. MANY OF THEM STAND UP AS WELL AS THE BEATLES.' **TIM RICE**

'ABBA WERE POP MUSIC IN ITS PUREST FORM. MOST AMERICANS HAD NO IDEA THEY WERE SWEDISH, EVEN WHEN THEY WENT TO No.1! MY FAVOURITE TRACK HAS TO BE "DANCING QUEEN" – IT WAS BACK THEN AND IT STILL IS TODAY.' **TINA TURNER**

'IT WAS VERY UNFASHIONABLE TO LIKE ABBA AT THAT TIME. THEIR SONGS ARE BEAUTIFULLY CRAFTED AND THE PRODUCTION WAS ALWAYS IMMACULATE, EVERYTHING BEAUTIFULLY TUNED IN TIME, AND THE GIRLS' VOICES WERE FABULOUS.' **BRIAN MAY**

'ABBA'S RECORDS REMAIN MASTERPIECES. EVEN AFTER ALL THESE YEARS, THEY'RE AS FRESH AS EVER. THEIR SONGWRITING AND PRODUCTION ARE IN A CLASS BY THEMSELVES. I HAVE HAD THE PLEASURE OF MEETING ABBA SEVERAL TIMES, AND I WILL ALWAYS CHERISH THE MEMORIES.' **NEIL SEDAKA**

'ABBA SAVED MY LIFE, IT'S UNDENIABLE. *ARRIVAL* IS A HAPPY RECORD. "DANCING QUEEN" IS THE BIGGEST SONG IN POP-MUSIC HISTORY, PURE ECSTASY, IT MAKES YOU WANT TO FLY.'   **BJÖRK**

'ABBA HAVE WRITTEN THE BEST POP MUSIC OF ALL TIME.' **THE EDGE** U2

'BJÖRN AND BENNY WERE MASTERS OF MELODIES AND LYRICS. THEY REPRESENT THE OLD SCHOOL OF COMPOSERS. THEY MADE PURE, SIMPLE AND INCOMPARABLE POP SONGS.' **SHARLEEN SPITERI** TEXAS

'THEY WERE THE ONLY GROUP THAT SET MY SPINE TINGLING. THEY MADE GREAT POP TUNES THAT HAVE STOOD THE TEST OF TIME.'   **ANDY BELL** ERASURE

ACKNOWLEDGEMENTS

I dedicate this book to my mother, Oscarine, and my grandmother, Augustine.

My heartfelt thanks go to Thierry Lecuyer for his support throughout this project.

I particularly want to thank the following: Philippe Elan for his invaluable help, his optimism and support at times of doubt and discouragement, and for his friendship; Rod Campbell for his advice and for supervising the translation; Görel Hanser for being so helpful and for giving me access to ABBA's photographic archive; Ingemar Bergman of Polar Music; Rune Söderqvist; and Colin Collier.

Thank you to Aurum Press for having believed in this project, particularly Karen Ings and Graham Eames, whose enthusiasm and professionalism made *Abba: The Book* a reality. It has been a pleasure working with you. Thanks also to Graham Peake and the team at TWO:design for their excellent work on the design of the book.

I would also like to thank all those who assisted me in my research and gave up their time so freely: Lillemor Andersson (Pressens Bild), Géraldine Atlani, Eddy Becker, Åsa Bergold (Polar Music), Alain Boublil, Torbjörn Calvero, Gilles Colombani, Kathryn Courtney-O'Neill, Bernard Deman, Philippe Denis, Annette Falck (IMS Bildbyrå), Lars Falck, Frédéric Fontbonne, Gunilla Gunnerheim (Folkparkerna), Johan Hellekant, Catherine Hinard, Johan Hjertberg, Bo Jensen, Helga van de Kar, Anita Notenboom and René Nieuwlaat (Agnetha, Benny, Björn, Frida Fan Club), Marc Krantz, Ola Lager, Patrick Largeteau, Michael Leckebusch, David Legrand, Sandrine Martin (RTL), Jean-Claude Misse, Alex Mizrahi, Bob Navez (Vogue Belgium), Thomas Nordin, Jokke Norling, Håkan Nygren, Tomas Nyh (EMA-Telstar), Jean Pajot, Carl Magnus Palm, Sven Åke Peterson (EMI Svenska AB), Phillip (PM ART), Jean-Michel Poncelet, Olle Rönnbäck (Polar Music), Marie-Laure Sanchez, Ivan Sandell, Hervé Tete, Vogue France.

Last, but not least, thank you to Agnetha, Björn, Benny and Anni-Frid for their remarkable talent and the pleasure their music has given me since 6 April 1974.

SOURCES

Books

Från Abba till Mamma Mia!, Carl Magnus Palm and Anders Hanser (Premium Publishing, 1999)
Abba Människorna och Musiken, Carl Magnus Palm (Tiden, 1996)
Som Jag Är, Agnetha Fältskog with Brita Åhman (Norstedts, 1996; translated into English as *As I Am*, Virgin, 1997)
Abba: The Complete Recording Sessions, Carl Magnus Palm (Century 22, 1994)
Abba: The Music Still Goes On, Paul Snaith (Castle Communications, 1994)
Abba Gold: The Complete Story, John Tobler (Century 22, 1993)
Stikkan: Den Börsnoterade Refrängsångaren, Oscar Hedlund (Sweden Music Förlag, 1983)
Abba In Their Own Words, Rosemary York (Omnibus Press, 1982)
Abba For the Record, John Tobler (Stafford Pemberton, 1980)
Succé På Världs-scenen, Leif Schulman and Charles Hammarsten (Allerbok, 1979)
Abba, Harry Edgington and Peter Himmelstrand (Magnum Books, 1979)
Bogen Om Abba, Rud Kofoed (Chr. Erichsens Forlag, 1977)
Abba By Abba, Christer Borg (Stafford Pemberton, 1977)

Newspapers and magazines

Abba Infos (Guy Bodescot), *Abba/International Magazine, Abba 5 Years, Aftonbladet, Allers, Arbetet, Bravo, Bild, Dagens Nyheter, Das Freizeit, Expressen, France-Soir, Hemmets, Juke Box, La Dernière Heure, Le Soir, Podium, Poster, Record Mirror, Salut, Saxons, Se, Svensk Damtidning, Télérama, Vecko Revyn.*

Television and films

Abba-Dabba-Dooo!!, Abba In Australia, Abba – The Movie, Aplauso, Dick Cavett Meets Abba, Gå På Vattnet Om Du Kan, Gäst Hos Hagge, Hylands Hörna, Made In Sweden For Export, Nöjesmaskinen, Raskenstam, Senoras y Senores, Stikkan Om Stikkan, Studio 2 – Abba In Poland, Thank You Abba, The Best of Abba – Musikladen, 300 Millones, Words and Music.

PICTURE CREDITS

Pressens Bild: pages 41 (left), 51, 52, 64, 66, 67, 72, 83, 85, 96, 98 (top and bottom), 100, 108 (centre), 139, 161 (bottom), 179, 195, 215, 224, 225, 240, 245 (top), 252, 255, 256
Kjell Johansson: pages 2, 44, 46, 65, 113 (top)
Stig Anderson collection: pages 8, 22, 23, 26, 36, 37, 38, 43, 60, 69, 87, 132, 134, 150, 153, 161 (left)
IMS Bildbyrå: pages 12, 14, 17, 18, 20, 24, 45, 47, 48, 49, 55, 58, 59, 68, 71, 74, 75, 104, 109 (right), 131, 133, 198, 199, 231, 238, 245 (bottom)
Lars Larsson (IMS Bildbyrå): pages 223, 227, 235, 250
Jean-Marie Potiez collection: pages 15, 16, 34, 50, 170, 171, 174, 182, 184, 205, 208
EMI Svenska: pages 29, 30 (top left), 30 (right), 40, 41 (right), 54
Polar Music: pages 32, 140, 142, 144, 147, 148, 151, 156, 158, 159, 162 (bottom), 163, 164, 166, 167, 168, 169, 175 (top), 186, 188, 190, 200, 212, 217
Jean Pajot: page 56
Premium Publishing: pages 78 (Bengt H. Malmqvist), 95, 129, 191 (Ola Lager), 178 (Torbjörn Calvero)
Bill Thomas: page 200, 202, 206, 207, 209, 211
Vogue Records: pages 86, 91, 110, 111, 113 (bottom), 116, 118, 123, 172, 183, 201, 218, 219, 232, 236, 243, 247
Camera Press: pages 89, 90, 106, 108 (left), 115, 175 (bottom)
Guido Marcon: pages 92, 112 (top and bottom)
Michael Leckebusch: pages 126 (top), 127, 128, 192
Phillipe Elan collection: pages 10, 30 (centre left), 62, 76, 77, 99, 102, 124, 137, 149, 187, 230
Ragnvi Gylder: page 81
PM Art Australia: pages 126 (centre and bottom), 130, 145
RCA: pages 154, 161 (right), 162 (top and centre)
Discomate: pages 180, 181, 213, 214

Every reasonable effort has been made to trace the copyright holders of the photographs in this book, but some were unreachable. Any photographer who has not been contacted is invited to write to the publishers in order that full acknowledgement can be made in future editions.